Iconic
Buildings

First published in the United States of America in 2017 by
Rizzoli International Publications, Inc.
300 Park Avenue South
New York, NY 10010
www.rizzoliusa.com

Originally published in the United Kingdom in 2017 by
RotoVision SA

2017 2018 2019 2020 / 10 9 8 7 6 5 4 3 2 1

ISBN: 978-0-7893-2770-3

Library of Congress Control Number: 2017942280

Printed in China

Publisher: Mark Searle
Editorial Director: Isheeta Mustafi
Commissioning Editor: Alison Morris
Junior Editor: Abbie Sharman
Design concept: Agata Rybicka
Layout: Ian Miller

Every effort has been made by the publishers to supply correct information on the buildings
included in this book. Any items marked with an asterisk (*) have very little information available
and the most reliable source found has been used. Sources are listed below.

Page 57 Architectuul.com

Iconic Buildings

AN ILLUSTRATED GUIDE TO THE WORLD'S
MOST REMARKABLE ARCHITECTURE

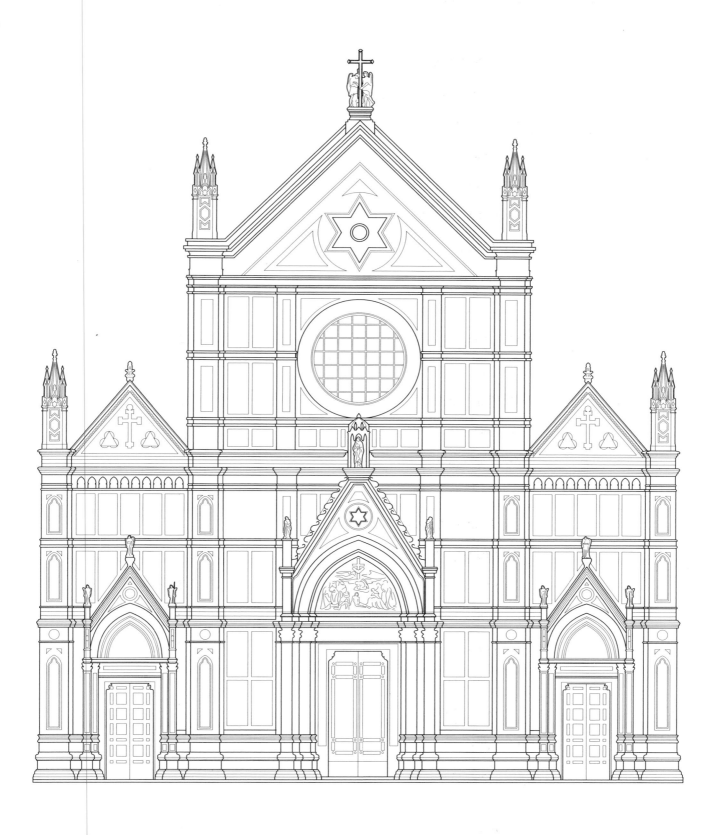

studio esinam

RIZZOLI
NEW YORK

New York · Paris · London · Milan

Contents

Introduction

Some of the first illustrations for this project were drawn in 2013. At the time we were working as an architect and art director respectively and had just founded studio esinam, a creative studio dedicated to exploring new ways of communicating architecture.

Our first project was called *Elevations* and was a series of art prints depicting buildings from different cities in the format of the architectural elevation drawing. By studying the facades and directing attention to details that often pass unseen, we hoped to reveal the qualities of the architecture that contribute to the unique atmosphere of each city. The first city was Paris (page 32), followed by Tokyo (page 72) and Berlin (page 46).

Over the years that followed, the collection grew and eventually we crossed paths with Mark Searle, publisher at RotoVision. He discovered our prints in a small design shop in Brighton and reached out to us with the proposition of making this book. The book offers a unique perspective on some of the world's most iconic buildings along with some lesser-known architectural gems. The eclectic collection of buildings exhibits a broad spectrum of architectural styles and vernaculars from the past millennia, from the ruins of the Forum Romanum and the Pantheon (page 40), to the contemporary minimalism of Tokyo (page 72), and the glass towers of Dubai (page 60).

The drawings are accompanied by basic architectural facts and information, with the aim to provide a deeper understanding of these amazing buildings.

We hope that this book will provide you with a fresh view on some of your favorite buildings, as well as introduce you to a few new ones.

—Josefine Lilljegren and Sebastian Gokah, founders of studio esinam

SANTA MARIA DEL FIORE (IL DUOMO DI FIRENZE), FLORENCE, PAGE 38

BAB AGNAOU, MARRAKECH, PAGE 24

CHRYSLER BUILDING, NEW YORK, PAGE 8

New York

1.

2.

3.

4.

5.

1. ONE WORLD TRADE CENTER
2. SOLOMON R. GUGGENHEIM MUSEUM
3. THE HIGH LINE 4. WOOLWORTH BUILDING
5. STATUE OF LIBERTY

New York has one of the most iconic skylines in the world. The high density of skyscrapers and tall buildings, created in just over 100 years, is testimony to the economic power of the city. Spreading over half of Manhattan Island, the story of this famous set of buildings starts in 1621 with a Dutch colony called New Amsterdam that comprised forts, homes, farms and government buildings located in what is now the tip of lower Manhattan. By 1664 it had been taken over by the British, renamed New York, and established as a port city. The city's most important development came with the advent of skyscrapers which were built in the early 1900s, and included the Gothic Revival style of the Woolworth Building, clad in stone; then came the Art Deco style of the Chrysler Building, clad in metal. Now glass facades, like that of One World Trade Center, are the most common sight.

1. ONE WORLD TRADE CENTER

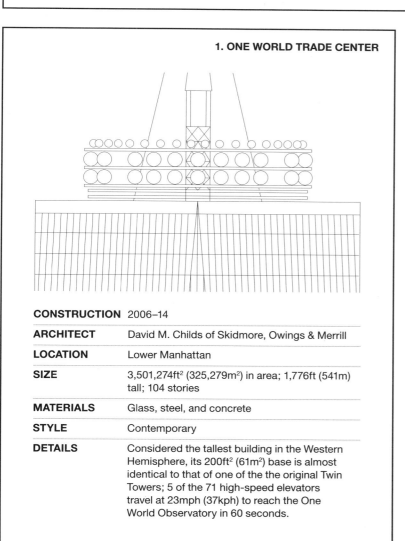

CONSTRUCTION	2006–14
ARCHITECT	David M. Childs of Skidmore, Owings & Merrill
LOCATION	Lower Manhattan
SIZE	3,501,274ft² (325,279m²) in area; 1,776ft (541m) tall; 104 stories
MATERIALS	Glass, steel, and concrete
STYLE	Contemporary
DETAILS	Considered the tallest building in the Western Hemisphere, its 200ft² (61m²) base is almost identical to that of one of the the original Twin Towers; 5 of the 71 high-speed elevators travel at 23mph (37kph) to reach the One World Observatory in 60 seconds.

2. SOLOMON R. GUGGENHEIM MUSEUM

CONSTRUCTION	1956–59
ARCHITECT	Frank Lloyd Wright
LOCATION	Fifth Avenue, Manhattan
SIZE	66,000ft² (6,131m²) in area; 92ft (28m) tall
MATERIALS	Concrete
STYLE	Modernist
DETAILS	Throughout the design process it was not obvious that the museum would be white; Wright first proposed red marble and brick. The ramp spiraling from the ground floor to the skylight dome is 1,416ft (432m) long.

5. STATUE OF LIBERTY

CONSTRUCTION	Started 1876 (sculpture) and 1881 (pedestal)
ARCHITECT	Frédéric Auguste Bartholdi (sculptor), Eugène Viollet-le-Duc and Gustave Eiffel (internal support), and Richard Morris Hunt (pedestal)
LOCATION	Liberty Island
SIZE	305ft (93m) high including pedestal
MATERIALS	Copper sheet with steel frame
STYLE	Neoclassical
DETAILS	The statue was a gift from the French people to celebrate freedom. The sculpture is hollow, and once housed an observation deck in the crown.

3. THE HIGH LINE

CONSTRUCTION	Completed 1934 (rail line); 2009 (Section I); 2011 (Section II); 2014 (Section III)
ARCHITECT	Diller Scofidio + Renfro (architect), James Corner Field Operations (landscape architect), and Piet Oudolf (planting designer)
LOCATION	West Side of Manhattan
SIZE	1.4mi (2.3km) long; 30ft (9m) above street level
MATERIALS	Steel, concrete, and plants
STYLE	Contemporary
DETAILS	The High Line is one of the world's most popular parks connected from disused rail lines in 2014, it attracts over 7 million visitors annually.

4. WOOLWORTH BUILDING

CONSTRUCTION	1910–13
ARCHITECT	Cass Gilbert
LOCATION	Lower Manhattan
SIZE	792ft (241m) tall; 60 stories
MATERIALS	Cast terra cotta cladding
STYLE	Gothic Revival
DETAILS	The tallest building in the world until 1930, when both the Chrysler Building and 40 Wall Street (the Trump Building) were completed.

CHRYSLER BUILDING

CONSTRUCTION	1928–30
ARCHITECT	William Van Alen
LOCATION	Lexington Avenue, Manhattan
SIZE	1,196,958ft² (111,201m²) in area; 1,046ft (318.9m) tall; 77 stories
MATERIALS	Brick and stainless steel
STYLE	Art Deco
DETAILS	It was once the world's tallest building until the Empire State Building opened 11 months later. The building is also unique due to parts of it being modeled on details of Chrysler cars—eagle heads jut out from the building and the radiator caps have the classic wing design.

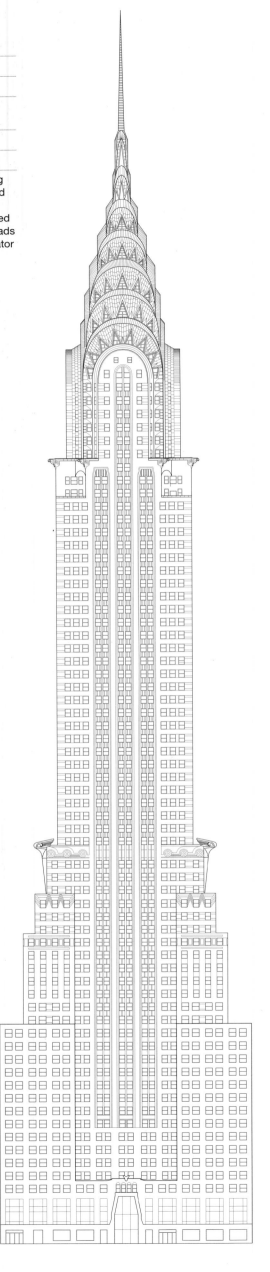

EMPIRE STATE BUILDING

CONSTRUCTION	1930–31
ARCHITECT	Shreve, Lamb, & Harmon
LOCATION	Fifth Avenue and 34th Street, Manhattan
SIZE	2.7 million ft² (250,838m²) of office space; 1,454ft (443m) tall; 102 floors
MATERIALS	Indiana limestone, granite, aluminum, and stainless steel
STYLE	Art Deco
DETAILS	Holding the record for the fastest construction for a project of its scale, it took just 1 year and 45 days to construct. It was the tallest building in the world for 41 years.

Los Angeles

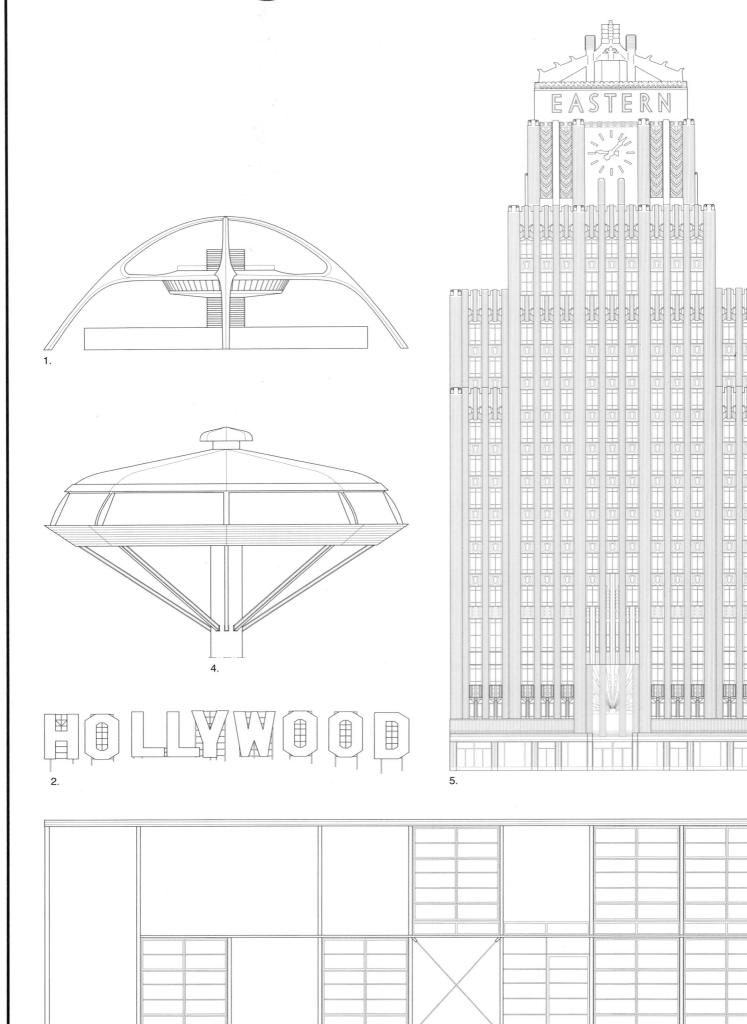

1. THEME BUILDING 2. HOLLYWOOD SIGN
3. EAMES HOUSE (CASE STUDY HOUSE NO. 8)
4. CHEMOSPHERE
5. EASTERN COLUMBIA BUILDING

The home of Hollywood and the center of the US film industry, Los Angeles is now the second-most populous city in the US. It was established in the 18th century as a small Spanish agricultural pueblo (town), with a central plaza, church, and market. The 20th century made it the sprawling, chaotic city it is today—international in style and population, accepting people and architecture from around the world.

Because of the high risk of earthquakes, LA's buildings are not as tall as in many other American cities. But like other American cities, its downtown architecture is a mixture of styles, from Classic Revival, Beaux Arts, and Art Deco, to midcentury modern, postmodern, contemporary—and the whimsical (but fast-disappearing) Googie architecture.

1. THEME BUILDING

CONSTRUCTION	Completed in 1961 (original design)
ARCHITECT	Pereira & Luckman Architects, Paul Revere Williams & Associates, and Welton Becket & Associates
LOCATION	Los Angeles International Airport, 1d Center Way
SIZE	105ft (32m) long; 107ft (32.6m) wide; 135ft (41m) tall
MATERIALS	Stucco-covered steel and concrete
STYLE	Neo-futurist, midcentury modern
DETAILS	The initial design had a glass dome as the airport's central hub. In 1997, Walt Disney Imagineering completed their earthquake resistant redesign of the interior and exterior.

2. HOLLYWOOD SIGN

CONSTRUCTION	Completed 1923
ARCHITECT	Thomas Fisk Goff for real estate developer H. J. Whitley
LOCATION	Mount Lee in Griffith Park
SIZE	Each letter is between 33ft (10m) and 40ft (12m) wide and 45ft (14m) tall; whole sign is 350ft (110m) long
MATERIALS	Steel
STYLE	Free-standing sign
DETAILS	The temporary sign was built to advertise a new housing development, but it soon became an international symbol of American film.

3. EAMES HOUSE (CASE STUDY HOUSE NO. 8)

CONSTRUCTION	Completed 1949
ARCHITECT	Charles and Ray Eames
LOCATION	203 North Chautauqua Boulevard, Pacific Palisades
SIZE	1,500ft^2 (139m^2) in area; studio: 1,000ft^2 (93m^2)
MATERIALS	Steel, glass, and wood
STYLE	Modernist
DETAILS	Designed and constructed by the legendary husband-and-wife team to serve as their home and studio. It was sponsored by *Arts & Architecture* magazine.

4. CHEMOSPHERE

CONSTRUCTION	Completed 1960
ARCHITECT	John Lautner
LOCATION	7776 Torreyson Drive, West Hollywood
SIZE	2,200ft^2 (204m^2) in area
MATERIALS	Concrete, steel, wood, and glass
STYLE	Midcentury modern
DETAILS	The building was named after the Chem Seal Corporation, one of the project's sponsors. They provided the resins and coatings used in the construction.

5. EASTERN COLUMBIA BUILDING

CONSTRUCTION	Completed 1930
ARCHITECT	Claud Beelman
LOCATION	849 South Broadway
SIZE	264ft (80m) tall; 13 stories
MATERIALS	Steel-reinforced concrete, clad in turquoise terra-cotta, with a blue-and-gold terra-cotta trim
STYLE	Art Deco
DETAILS	Originally the headquarters for the Eastern Outfitting Company and the Columbia Outfitting Company. It is considered to be one of the finest surviving examples of Art Deco architecture in the city.

WALT DISNEY CONCERT HALL

CONSTRUCTION	1999–2003
ARCHITECT	Frank O. Gehry/Gehry Partners
LOCATION	111 South Grand Avenue, Los Angeles
SIZE	200,000ft^2 (60,960m^2) in area
MATERIALS	Stainless steel
STYLE	Deconstructivist
DETAILS	Home of the Los Angeles Philharmonic, the bold exterior gives way to the 2,265-seat, Douglas fir-lined hall, which is considered to be one of the acoustically-finest concert halls in the world.

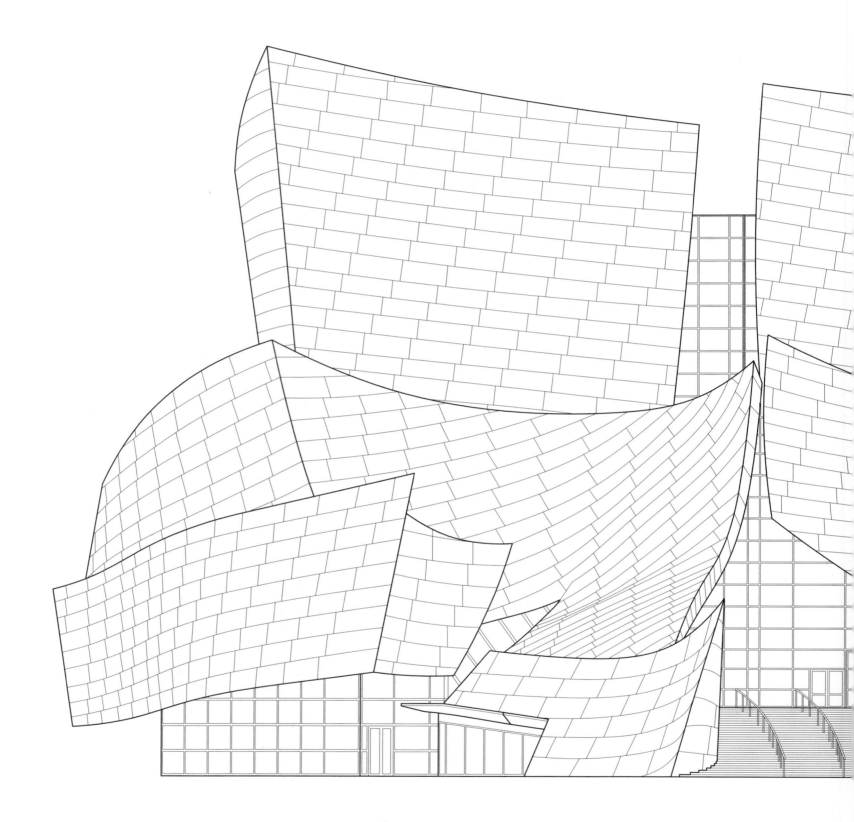

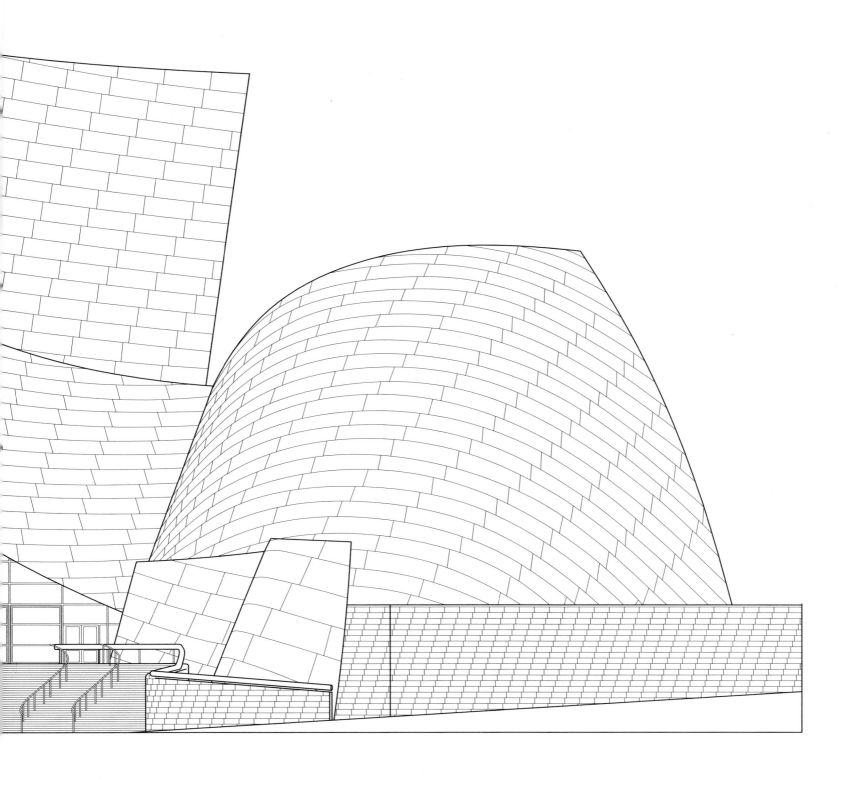

Washington, DC

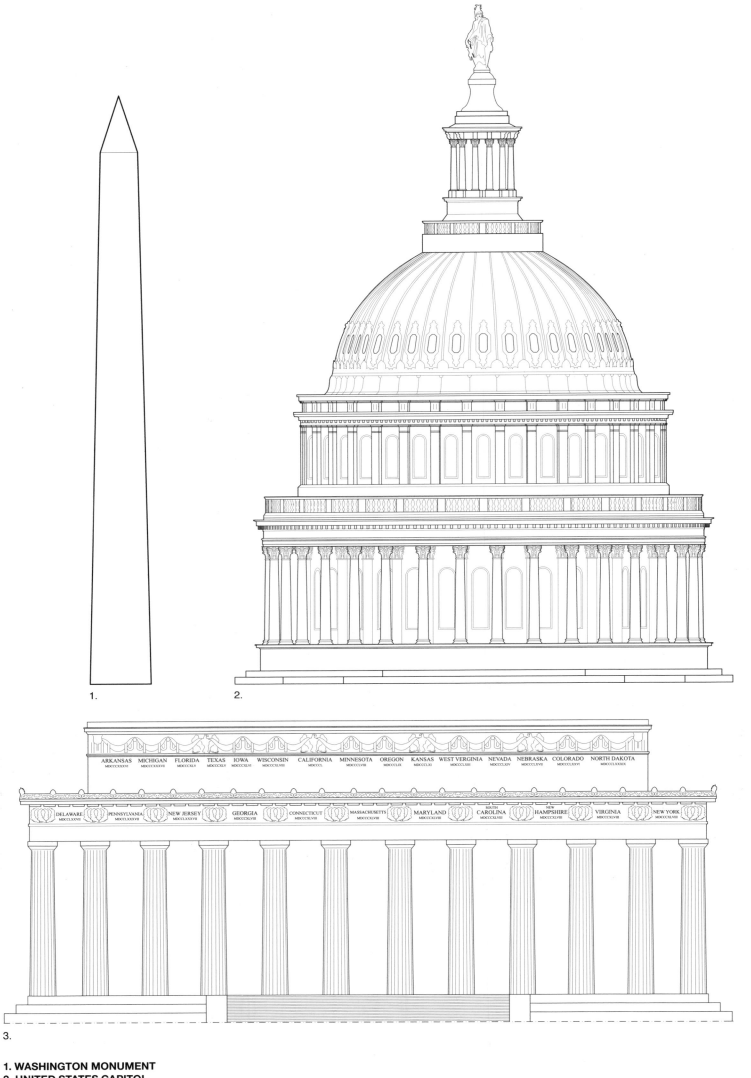

1. WASHINGTON MONUMENT
2. UNITED STATES CAPITOL
3. LINCOLN MEMORIAL

The capital of the United States, Washington DC is a 68.3mi² (177km²) federal district along the Potomac and Anacostia Rivers between Maryland and Virginia. While it has a city government, the District is under the jurisdiction of the US Congress. Officially founded in 1790 as the permanent seat of the federal government, the site was selected by—and named after—George Washington, the first American president.

Pierre Charles L'Enfant, a French-born architect and city planner, is credited as the overall master-planner of the new city. Much of Washington was burned by the British in the War of 1812, including the White House and the US Capitol. The centerpiece of L'Enfant's plan was a grand boulevard, now the National Mall. The two-mile park stretches from the Capitol to the Lincoln Memorial, and includes the Washington Monument, several memorials, and Smithsonian museums. The White House is technically not a part of the Mall, but is connected by President's Park.

The gamut of architectural styles that characterize this low-rise city includes everything from Neoclassical, Beaux Arts, and Gothic Revival, to Georgian, Victorian, and Modern. The oldest original and surviving structure in Washington is The Old Stone House that dates back to 1765 and is located in historic Georgetown, famous for its cobbled streets, picturesque canal, and some of the oldest architecture in the city.

1. WASHINGTON MONUMENT

CONSTRUCTION	1848–84
ARCHITECT	Original design by Robert Mills and final design by Thomas Lincoln Casey Sr.
LOCATION	National Mall
SIZE	55ft (17m) long; 55ft (17m) wide; and 555ft (169m) high
MATERIALS	Marble, granite, sandstone, aluminum, and cast iron
STYLE	Egyptian Obelisk
DETAILS	Inside the monument is an open shaft with an elevator and stairs to the top. Renovation of the monument will be completed in 2019.

2. UNITED STATES CAPITOL

CONSTRUCTION	1793–1813
ARCHITECT	William Thornton and Benjamin Henry Latrobe (1793–1818); Charles Bulfinch (restoration 1818–29); and Thomas U. Walter (1850 expansion plan)
LOCATION	Capitol Hill
SIZE	751ft (228.9m) long; 350ft (107m) wide; 288ft (88m) tall
MATERIALS	Sandstone, marble, brick, and cast iron
STYLE	Neoclassical
DETAILS	The painted cast iron dome mimics the stone used for the building below. After a three-year restoration, the scaffolding came down in time for the 2017 Presidential Inauguration ceremony.

3. LINCOLN MEMORIAL

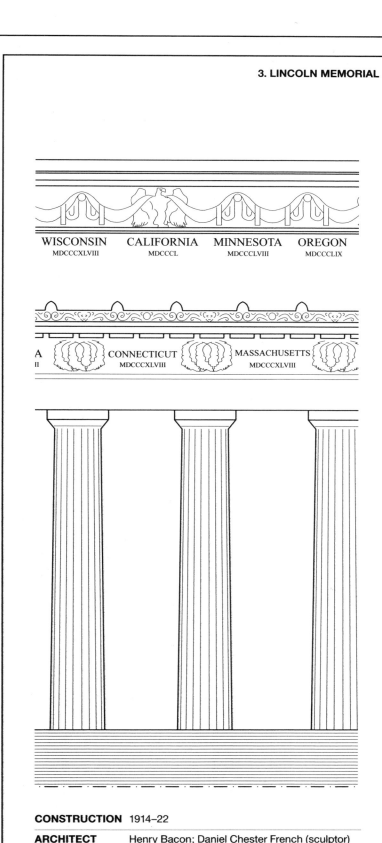

CONSTRUCTION	1914–22
ARCHITECT	Henry Bacon; Daniel Chester French (sculptor)
LOCATION	Lincoln Memorial Circle, National Mall
SIZE	202ft (62m) long; 132ft (40m) wide; 99ft (30m) tall
MATERIALS	Marble, granite, limestone, and copper alloy
STYLE	Greek Revival
DETAILS	Built to honor the 16th president of the United States. In 1963, Martin Luther King Jr. made his "I Have a Dream" speech on the steps.

Montréal

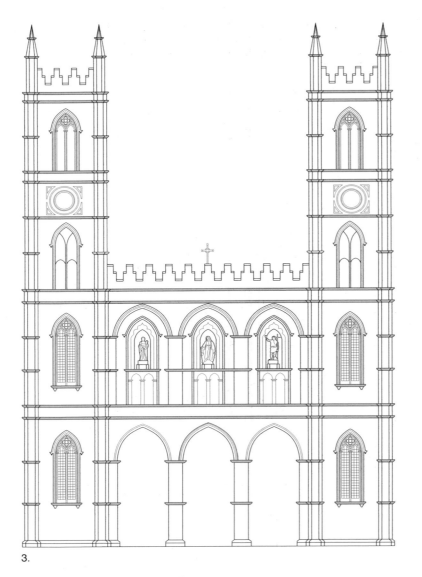

3.

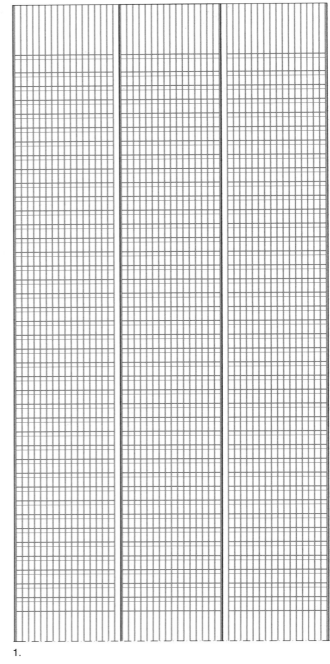

1.

2.

1. PLACE VILLE MARIE
2. HABITAT 67
3. NOTRE-DAME BASILICA OF MONTRÉAL

Montréal, an island city, is one of the most important and densely populated cities in Canada. It is also the most important francophone city in Québec. French explorers colonized the city and its history began with French fur merchants in the 18th century. However, it was the industrial era that really allowed it to grow and develop into a manufacturing city. Most of the industrial buildings lie on the outskirts of the city center, leaving the island area as a charismatic French–English city with smaller-scale housing boroughs and high-rise business districts. One of the defining characteristics of the housing district is the three-story terrace houses with outdoor staircases, which give the streets and neighborhoods of the district an individual style.

Since the late 19th century, Montréal has been developing the cultural and business center of the city located downtown. Although there is still a showcase of architecture from this period, skyscrapers are thriving and have replaced some of the city's more historic buildings.

Montréal, with its extreme winters, has the largest underground city in the world. The first underground development was designed by I. M. Pei as the Ville Marie shopping center, which connected to the metro station. It quickly developed, with connecting metro stations and new underground buildings, and has transformed Montréal with more than 190 entrances, stores, and hotels.

1. PLACE VILLE MARIE

CONSTRUCTION	1955–62
ARCHITECT	I. M. Pei and Henry N. Cobb
LOCATION	Downtown Montréal
SIZE	1,032,500ft² (95,922m²) in area; 617ft (188m) tall; 42 stories
MATERIALS	Steel, concrete, aluminum, and glass
STYLE	International Style
DETAILS	Light from the rotating beacon on top of the building is visible from as far away as 31mi (50km).

2. HABITAT 67

CONSTRUCTION	Completed 1967
ARCHITECT	Moshe Safdie
LOCATION	Cité du Havre
SIZE	12 stories; 354 600ft² (56m²) in area modules combined into 146 units
MATERIALS	Prefabricated concrete
STYLE	Brutalist
DETAILS	The complex, built for Expo 67 as a prototype for multifamily housing, is a model of prefab, modular construction, with apartments ranging from 600ft² (56m²) to 1,700ft² (158m²).

3. NOTRE-DAME BASILICA OF MONTRÉAL

CONSTRUCTION	1824–29
ARCHITECT	James O'Donnell; and John Ostell (twin towers, 1843)
LOCATION	Downtown Montréal
SIZE	200ft (60m) tall
MATERIALS	Stone
STYLE	Gothic Revival
DETAILS	The basilica houses the great bell, Jean-Baptiste, which weighs 11t (11,000kg). It was cast in England and raised into position using cables and pulley blocks that were borrowed from a railroad company.

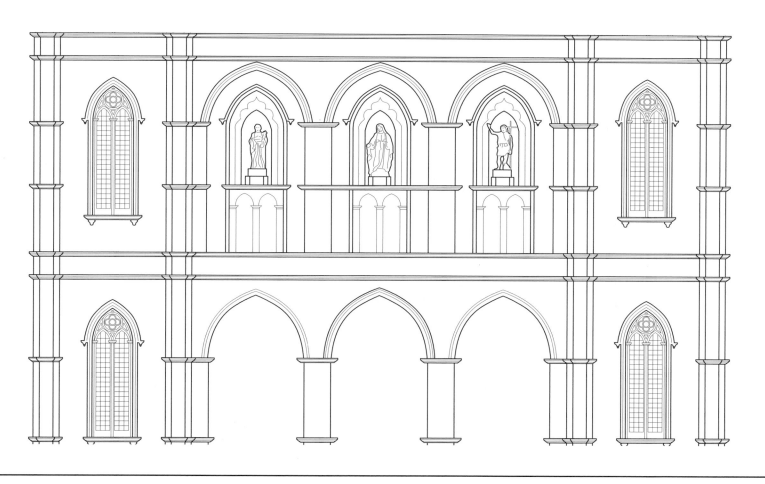

Vancouver

1.

2.

3.

1. SCIENCE WORLD AT TELUS WORLD OF SCIENCE
2. HARBOUR CENTRE 3. DOMINION BUILDING

Vancouver is a relatively new city, developed only in the late 1800s thanks largely to the north coast railroad and the gold rush. Its architecture is testimony of this somewhat recent development. However, aboriginal peoples roamed the area for more than 3,000 years before the first European settlers arrived. The architecture here bears witness to the city's more recent development and the blend of cultures gives Vancouver its identity as one of the most ethnically diverse cities in Canada.

The sea on three sides and the high mountains in the north give Vancouver a geographical characteristic that few cities can provide. The old city is a peninsula within another peninsula, which is protected on the west by the Island of Vancouver and makes it the warmest place in Canada. Its important location, the port and rail of the west coast, and its vicinity to the American state of Washington have made the city an economic hub. The city is also well known for being a hub for sports and culture, boasting a biodiversity center and an anthropology museum as well as the Olympic Winter Games site and stadiums.

1. SCIENCE WORLD AT TELUS WORLD OF SCIENCE

CONSTRUCTION	1986 (original Expo Centre opening), 1989 (completion of expansion)
ARCHITECT	Bruno Freschi (original architect); Buckminster Fuller (geodesic dome design); Boak Alexander (architect of expansion)
LOCATION	1455 Quebec Street
SIZE	109,792ft^2 (10,200m^2) in area; 155ft (47m) tall
MATERIALS	Aluminum
STYLE	Modernism–Futurism
DETAILS	Designed for Expo 86 and later refurbished as a science hub.

2. HARBOUR CENTRE

CONSTRUCTION	1974–77
ARCHITECT	WZMH Architects
LOCATION	555 West Hastings Street
SIZE	594,172ft^2 (55,200m^2) in area; 581ft (177m) tall; 28 stories plus observation deck
MATERIALS	Concrete
STYLE	Modernist
DETAILS	Officially opened by astronaut Neil Armstrong, the UFO-like structure atop the tower includes a revolving restaurant and an observation deck. The 100ft (30m) antenna is festooned with bright red lights for the Christmas season.

3. DOMINION BUILDING

CONSTRUCTION	1908–10
ARCHITECT	J. S. Helyer and Son
LOCATION	207 West Hastings Street
SIZE	148ft (45m) tall; 13 stories
MATERIALS	Steel frame, brick, stone, and terra cotta
STYLE	Beaux Arts
DETAILS	The trapezoidal building was the city's first steel-framed high-rise and until 1912 it was the tallest building in the British Empire. It is considered the crown jewel of Vancouver's heritage architecture.

Santiago

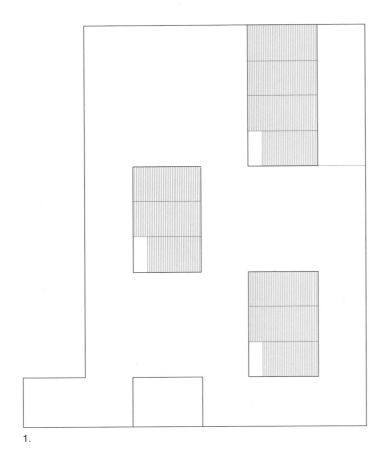

1.

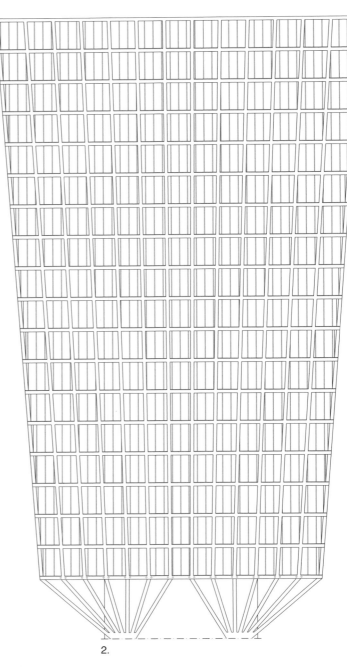

2.

3.

1. UC INNOVATION CENTER
2. CRUZ DEL SUR BUILDING
3. PALACIO DE LA MONEDA

Santiago, the capital of Chile, is situated at the center of the country in a valley irrigated by the Mapocho River. The country itself is a long, narrow stretch of land between the Pacific Ocean and the Andes mountain range. This geography, with hot summers and mild winters, makes central Chile a very fertile region. Habitation is archaeologically known to go back more than 10,000 years, but the earliest settlements only date to the Incan era, some 100 years before the Spanish conquered the area.

Indigenous tribes that had settled before the Spanish conquest make up approximately 11% of Santiago's population today. There is a strong and interesting mix of traditions, from native pre-Hispanic events to Christian celebrations; vendimias are held annually to celebrate the grape harvest.

The city today is a hub of culture that is transforming into a modern city, respectful of its history and the environment. The old Plaza de Armas has been opened to create a lively square, enhancing its original characteristics and developing its potential as a center for the people. In the same way, La Moneda Palace has been refurbished with an underground parking lot and a civic center. Above it is a new plaza with gardens and terraces. The city spreads out and is divided into barrios, from its Spanish tradition. Each has its own identity and has developed in a different way, some from high-class residential areas and some from much poorer neighborhoods. For tourism and city life the neighborhoods around the central quarter have developed to offer culture, leisure, and nightlife.

1. UC INNOVATION CENTER

CONSTRUCTION	2012–14
ARCHITECT	Alejandro Aravena of Elemental
LOCATION	Vicuña Mackenna 4860, Macul, Santiago Metropolitan Region
SIZE	88,006ft² (8,176 m²) in area; 14 stories
MATERIALS	Concrete
STYLE	Contemporary
DETAILS	Three-stories-tall, deeply-recessed openings in the monolithic concrete facades circulate fresh air and provide terraces on several floors.

2. CRUZ DEL SUR BUILDING

CONSTRUCTION	2008–09
ARCHITECT	Izquierdo Lehmann Arquitectos
LOCATION	Apoquindo 4501-4549, Las Condes
SIZE	42,915ft² (3,987m²) in area; 21 stories
MATERIALS	Concrete and glass
STYLE	Contemporary
DETAILS	The building plays a "balancing act" as the facades cantilever out as they rise, supported on a concrete base.

3. PALACIO DE LA MONEDA

CONSTRUCTION	1784–1805
ARCHITECT	Joaquín Toesca
LOCATION	Civic District
SIZE	Unknown
MATERIALS	Stone, wood, metal, and brick
STYLE	Neoclassical
DETAILS	Currently the seat of the President of the Republic of Chilé, originally housing the national mint.

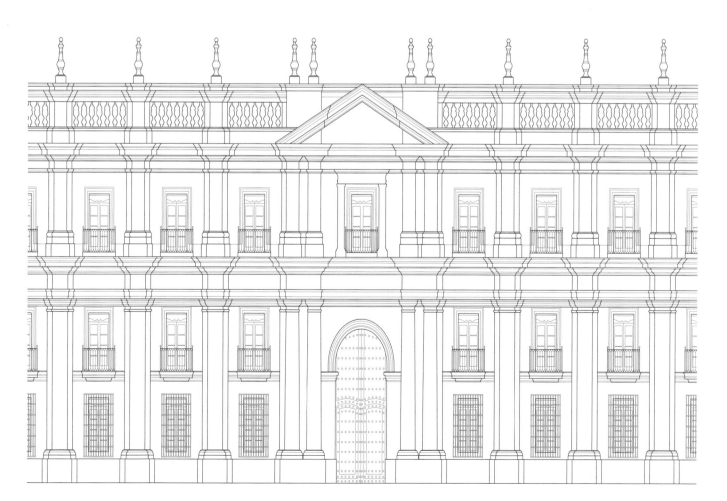

Rio de Janeiro

3.

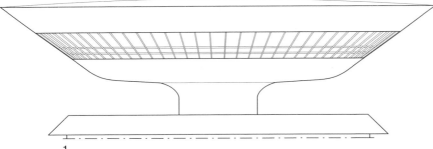

1.

4.

2.

1. NITERÓI CONTEMPORARY ART MUSEUM
2. CARIOCA AQUEDUCT
3. CHRIST THE REDEEMER
4. GRAN MELIÁ NACIONAL

Home to the huge statue of Christ the Redeemer atop Corcovado mountain, the city of Rio stretches out below, surrounded by rocky peaks on three sides and a beautiful beach along the coast. Nestled among these coastal mountains, nature balances the urban sprawl that boasts a wealth of architectural styles.

It has not always been like this. When the Portuguese expelled the French merchants in 1567 they settled into this tropical paradise. But poor planning and the challenging terrain meant that the city grew in a fairly haphazard manner. Swamps and lagoons were carelessly filled in to build houses and reclaim land for agriculture, and by the end of the 18th century, the ecosystem and population were so endangered that serious measurements had to be taken in order to avoid more epidemics and to provide fresh water to the city. This led to the construction of the Carioca Aqueduct.

In 1808 the Portuguese crown, feeling the threat of Napoléon, moved their capital from Lisbon to Rio. The transformation of Rio from colonial city to imperial capital changed the whole aspect of the city. Noble houses and palaces, government buildings, and a library to host the 60,000 books brought from Portugal were built. Later, in 1822, Brazil acquired its independence, but it wasn't until 1889 that it became a republic.

The 20th century brought new urban ideals, and the city was modernized: avenues were opened, unsafe buildings demolished, and reforestation had begun. But by the mid-1900s the industrial city, capital, and port were again plagued by overpopulation and unsustainable growth as newcomers settled on the hills around the city, creating the famous favelas. The capital was then moved to Brasilia in 1960 to slow further growth.

1. NITERÓI CONTEMPORARY ART MUSEUM

CONSTRUCTION	Completed 1996
ARCHITECT	Oscar Niemeyer
LOCATION	Niterói
SIZE	Exhibition space: 4,305ft^2 (400m^2) in area; 52.5ft (16m) tall; and 164ft (50m) in diameter
MATERIALS	Concrete and glass
STYLE	Modernist
DETAILS	Portuguese name: Museu de Arte Contemporânea de Niterói (MAC);set on a cliff top the museum rests on a pedestal hovering over an 8,790ft^2 (817m^2) reflecting pool overlooking Guanabara Bay and Sugarloaf Mountain.

2. CARIOCA AQUEDUCT

CONSTRUCTION	Completed 1750
ARCHITECT	José Fernandes Pinto Alpoim
LOCATION	Lapa
SIZE	885ft (270m) long
MATERIALS	Stone
STYLE	Romanesque
DETAILS	Today the 42-arch structure serves as a bridge for the historic Santa Teresa tram.

4. GRAN MELIÁ NACIONAL

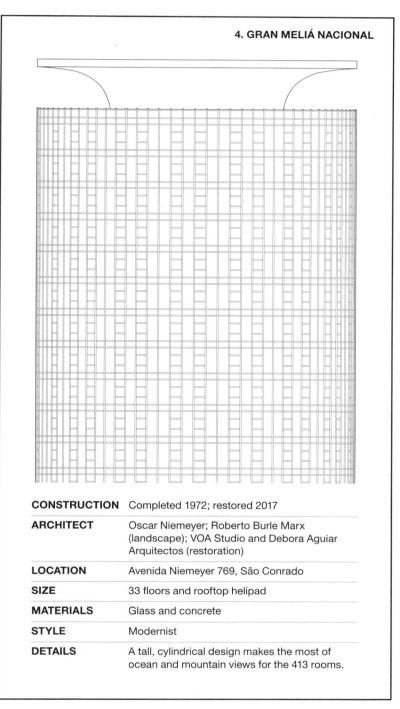

CONSTRUCTION	Completed 1972; restored 2017
ARCHITECT	Oscar Niemeyer; Roberto Burle Marx (landscape); VOA Studio and Debora Aguiar Arquitectos (restoration)
LOCATION	Avenida Niemeyer 769, São Conrado
SIZE	33 floors and rooftop helipad
MATERIALS	Glass and concrete
STYLE	Modernist
DETAILS	A tall, cylindrical design makes the most of ocean and mountain views for the 413 rooms.

3. CHRIST THE REDEEMER

CONSTRUCTION	1922–31
ARCHITECT	Paul Landowski and Gheorghe Leonida(sculptors); Heitor da Silva Costa and Albert Caquot (engineers)
LOCATION	Mount Corcovado
SIZE	124ft (37m) tall (including base); 92ft (28m) arm span
MATERIALS	Reinforced concrete and soapstone tiles
STYLE	Art Deco
DETAILS	Considered the fifth-tallest statue of Jesus in the world, the sculpture sits atop a 2,330ft (710m) mountain overlooking the city.

Marrakech

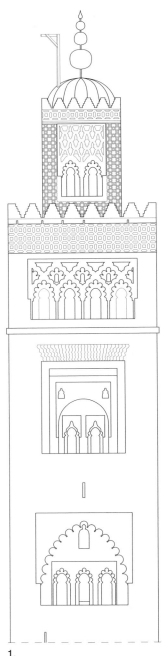

2.

1.

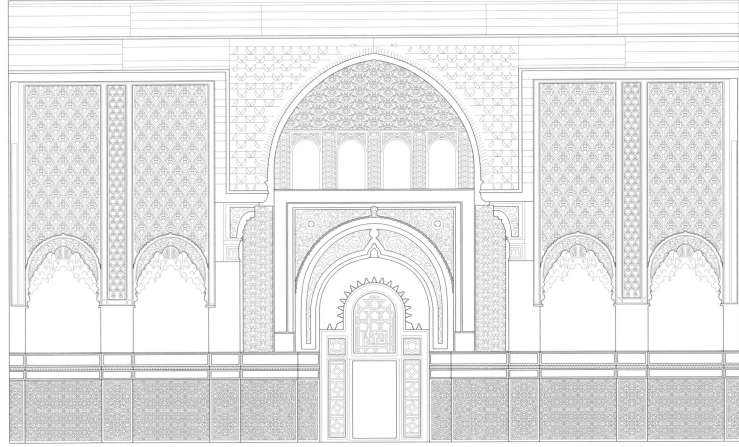

3.

1. KOUTOUBIA MOSQUE
2. BAB AGNAOU
3. BEN YOUSSEF MADRASA

Marrakech is an Islamic city in Morocco founded by the Almoravid dynasty in the early 12th century after they had conquered the northwest of Africa and the south of Spain. Marrakech was established as the empire's capital and artisans from the Spanish cities of Andalucia were brought in to build the first mosque and palace. Some of the most important works of this period include the city's red ramparts and the underground canals.

The city, an old oasis, is still protected by the ramparts that have now been extended south and west. The original 12th-century structures give a very impressive aspect to the city as a whole, especially from the southwest where the snowcapped Atlas Mountains can be seen in the background.

The 12th century saw the Almohad dynasty build some of the largest mosques in the western part of the Muslim empire. All mosques are built to have a courtyard, ablution fountains, and a minaret or tower. The construction of a mosque adheres to strict rules, and generally follows the same layout as the Masjid an-Nabawi in Medina, built by the Prophet Muhammad on the site of his house.

When the ruling dynasty fell at the end of the 14th century the city remained largely unchanged until the 16th century, when the wealthy Sultan Ahmed El Mansour took over the city and built the el-Badi Palace.

The beauty of the city lies in its natural environment, its red clay, and the splendor of its Islamic architecture. The extremely detailed architecture links the interior and exterior spaces with perforated walls that give access to wind and light, creating intricate geometric patterns on walls and floors.

1. KOUTOUBIA MOSQUE

CONSTRUCTION	12th century (*ca.* 1150–99)
ARCHITECT	Completion overseen by Caliph Abu Yusuf Ya'qub al-Mansur
LOCATION	Avenue Mohammed V
SIZE	Base: 58,000ft^2 (5,400m^2) in area; minaret 253ft (77m) tall
MATERIALS	Brick, sandstone, and ceramic tiles
STYLE	Almohad
DETAILS	The largest mosque in Marrakech, the prayer hall can hold 25,000 worshippers.

2. BAB AGNAOU

CONSTRUCTION	12th century (ca.1121–1269)
ARCHITECT	Overseen by Caliph Abu Yusuf Yaqub al-Mansur
LOCATION	Rue Moulay Ismail
SIZE	19ft (5.8m) high
MATERIALS	Stone and brick
STYLE	Almohad
DETAILS	One of the most notable of the walled city's 19 gates, it originally served as the entrance to the Royal Casbah.

3. BEN YOUSSEF MADRASA

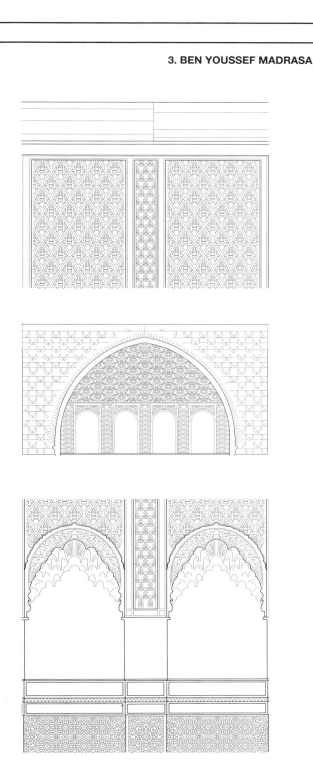

CONSTRUCTION	14th century; reconstructed in 1564
ARCHITECT	16th-century reconstruction overseen by Sultan Abdallah al-Ghalib (1557–74)
LOCATION	Kaat Benahid
SIZE	19,000ft^2 (1,765m^2) in area
MATERIALS	Cedar, marble, stucco, and mosaic
STYLE	Moorish
DETAILS	Until it closed in 1960, this was one of the largest madrasas in North Africa, housing nearly 900 students. In 1982 it was restored and reopened to the public as a museum.

London

1. NELSON'S COLUMN 2. GEORGIAN TOWNHOUSES
3. MARBLE ARCH 4. ELIZABETH TOWER (BIG BEN)
5. ST PAUL'S CATHEDRAL

London is one of the largest and most cosmopolitan cities in Europe. Old and new architecture sit together, with growth not only in the suburbs, like many other capitals, but in the city center as well. Plans for new buildings and skyscrapers are submitted every year; however, once building work is approved, a period of time may be allowed for rescue archaeology to take place before new construction is started.

The city of Londinium was founded soon after the Roman invasion in 43 CE and is thought to have been only a square mile in area (2.6km²). It is now the site of the modern City of London, otherwise known as The Square Mile, home to the city's financial and trading industry.

London has undergone many changes and developments, with the Great Fire of 1666 destroying most of the city's timber buildings. Much of the city, including St. Paul's Cathedral, had to be rebuilt as a result. However, the biggest notable growth of London took place during the Victorian era. Examples of the Gothic Revival architecture of this period can be seen in the Palace of Westminster, St. Pancras Railway Station, and Tower Bridge.

The London Underground is the world's first subterranean railway system and started with the Metropolitan Railway in 1863. It now comprises 270 stations over roughly 250 miles (400km) of track that run through the city and connect it to adjacent counties.

1. NELSON'S COLUMN

CONSTRUCTION	1840–43
ARCHITECT	William Railton (column); Edward Hodges Baily (statue); and Edwin Landseer and Carlo Marochetti (bronze lions, 1867)
LOCATION	Trafalgar Square
SIZE	187ft (57m) tall; column: 169ft (52m) tall; statue: 18ft (5m) tall
MATERIALS	Granite and bronze
STYLE	Corinthian column
DETAILS	The statue depicts Admiral Horatio Nelson, commanding officer of the Royal Navy who died in the 1805 Battle of Trafalgar, off the coast of Spain where the British were ultimately victorious.

2. GEORGIAN TOWNHOUSES

CONSTRUCTION	1775–83
ARCHITECT	Various
LOCATION	Bedford Square
SIZE	3 floors with a servants' attic
MATERIALS	Brick
STYLE	Georgian
DETAILS	Some of the finest, best-preserved Georgian architecture in London surrounds a private central garden. Many of the buildings are now occupied by businesses and universities.

3. MARBLE ARCH

CONSTRUCTION	Completed 1833
ARCHITECT	John Nash (arch design); J. C. F. Rossi, Richard Westmacott, and Edward Hodges Baily (sculptures); and Samuel Parker (bronze gates)
LOCATION	Northeast corner of Hyde Park
SIZE	60ft (18m) wide; 30ft (9m) deep, 269ft (82m) tall
MATERIALS	Carrara marble
STYLE	Neoclassical
DETAILS	The arch originally marked the entrance to Buckingham Palace, but it was relocated in 1851 to form a ceremonial entrance to Hyde Park.

4. ELIZABETH TOWER (BIG BEN)

CONSTRUCTION	Completed 1859
ARCHITECT	Augustus Pugin and Charles Barry (clock tower); and Edmund Beckett Denison and Edward Dent (clock movement)
LOCATION	Palace of Westminster
SIZE	315ft (96m) tall; clock faces: 23ft (7m) in diameter
MATERIALS	Limestone-clad brick, opal glass, and cast-iron spire
STYLE	Gothic Revival
DETAILS	Though the tower is commonly called Big Ben, the name actually refers to the 13-ton bell. In 2012, Parliament renamed the structure Elizabeth Tower in honor of the Queen's Diamond Jubilee.

CONSTRUCTION	1675–1710
ARCHITECT	Christopher Wren
LOCATION	Ludgate Hill
SIZE	365ft (111m) tall
MATERIALS	Portland stone, bricks, iron, and wood
STYLE	English baroque
DETAILS	This is one of 52 churches that were rebuilt by Christopher Wren after the Great Fire of 1666. The cathedral survived the Blitz of 1940–41 but was subsequently bombed twice. Until the 1960s it remained the tallest building in London.

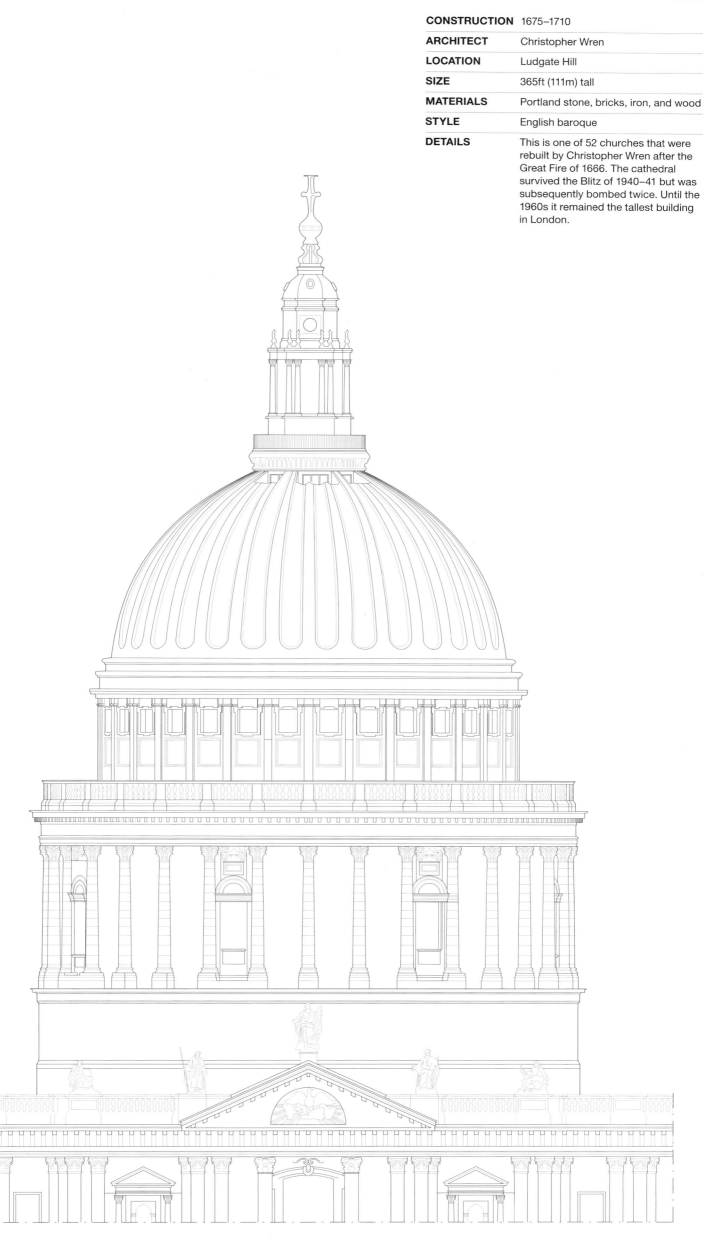

Barcelona

1.

2.

3.

1. CASA BATLLÓ
2. SAGRADA FAMILIA
3. BARCELONA PAVILION

This major city in the Catalan region of Spain bears witness to a long and rich history. Its Roman wall still holds strong in the area of San Jaume, and the Roman roads Cardo and Decumanus trace the principal axes within the ancient walls. The medieval Barrio Gótico (Gothic Quarter) is an intricate area of narrow streets with no sidewalks around the cathedral. Today many of the medieval buildings have been transformed into art shops or bars.

After a long period of change, uncertainty, and war, Barcelona grew slowly until the early 1800s, when a new port was developed and an era of industry and commerce began. Wealth created jobs and led to an expansion of the city and new areas of construction. The Plan Cerdá is an urban development named after Ildefons Cerdá in which the new city outside the medieval quarter was developed according to the grid structure, comprising 145yd (133m) square blocks with the corners cut off to give a better view of the crossings.

In the 19th and 20th centuries, architects embellished the city with a Catalan version of the architectural styles of Europe that came to be called Modernisme or Catalan Modernism. Key examples include Lluís Domènech i Montaner's Castell dels tres Dragons (Castle of the Three Dragons) and Antoni Gaudí's Sagrada Família, which is expected to be one of the largest temples in the world and is still under construction.

In recent years, famous modern architects have offered a contrast to Gaudí's architecture; the 1929 German Pavilion by Ludwig Mies Van der Rohe and Santiago Calatrava's Bac de Roda Bridge which was completed in 1987 are two notable examples.

1. CASA BATLLÓ

CONSTRUCTION	Completed 1877; redesign by Gaudí completed 1907
ARCHITECT	Antoni Gaudí
LOCATION	Passeig de Gràcia, 43
SIZE	46,285ft^2 (4,300m^2) in area; 105ft (32m) tall
MATERIALS	Sandstone, iron, wood, and colorful glass and ceramic mosaics
STYLE	Catalan modernism (also known as Catalan Art Nouveau)
DETAILS	With organic and symbolic forms, such as balconies that look like skulls, and window supports that look like bones, the house is also referred to as Casa dels Ossos (House of Bones). The roof terrace is encircled by what is considered to be the dragon slain by St. George, the patron saint of Barcelona.

2. SAGRADA FAMÍLIA

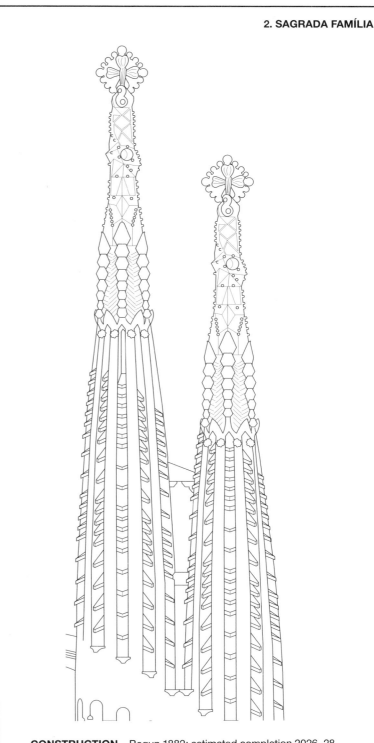

CONSTRUCTION	Begun 1882; estimated completion 2026–28
ARCHITECT	Antoni Gaudí and Jordi Faulí (appointed chief architect in 2012)
LOCATION	Plaça de la Sagrada Família
SIZE	When completed: 312ft (95m) long; 196ft (60m) wide; tallest tower: 560ft (170m)
MATERIALS	Sandstone, granite, brick, and concrete
STYLE	Catalan Art Nouveau, and Gothic
DETAILS	When Gaudí died in 1926, less than 25% of the project was completed. Today 70% of the work has been carried out, and it is estimated to be completed by 2026–28.

3. BARCELONA PAVILION

CONSTRUCTION	Completed 1929; demolished 1930; reconstructed 1986
ARCHITECT	Ludwig Mies van der Rohe
LOCATION	Avenida de Francesc Ferrer i Guàrdia, 7
SIZE	9,698ft^2 (901m^2) in area; 10ft (3m) tall; 1 story
MATERIALS	Glass, steel, concrete, four different types of marble, and onyx
STYLE	International Style
DETAILS	Originally designed as the German Pavilion for the 1929 Barcelona International Exhibition, and dismantled in 1930, it was rebuilt in 1986 using the same materials. It remains one of the most influential modernist buildings of the 20th century. Mies designed the still-popular Barcelona Chair for the pavilion.

Paris

1. PALAIS GARNIER 2. PONT MARIE
3. CENTRE POMPIDOU
4. SACRÉ COEUR
5. ARC DE TRIOMPHE DE L'ÉTOILE

The French capital, situated in the north of the country and straddling the Seine River, has 2,000 years of history. In 200 CE, under Roman rule, the Île de la Cité, a small island in the middle of the Seine, became Lutetia Civitas—city of Lutetia. Most of this past has been buried but one can still trace the Cardo (main north-south sheet) and remnants of its aqueduct. Medieval times brought Paris its first big expansion and saw it become the French capital. The beautiful gothic Sainte-Chapelle chapel and the Notre Dame Cathedral were placed in the center. The city grew toward the south, which is evidenced by the narrow, winding streets of Saint-Germain. Since then, the city has expanded into a semicircular pattern with Notre Dame at its heart.

Paris is widely known as one of the most beautiful cities in Europe. This beauty comes from a uniformity in the scale of its buildings. In the mid-1800s Baron Haussmann, a politician in charge of the urban development of Paris under Napoléon III's rule, set up the parameters to reorganize the city using neoclassical ideas. Everything from parks to train stations was rebuilt or refurbished to align the buildings. In 1977, a height regulation of 121 feet (37 meters) for buildings was put in place to avoid unsightly skyscrapers. This has now been relaxed to accommodate a growing urban population.

1. PALAIS GARNIER

CONSTRUCTION	1861–65
ARCHITECT	Charles Garnier
LOCATION	8 rue Scribe, Place de l'Opéra
SIZE	568ft (173m) long; 410ft (125m) wide; 240ft (73m) tall; 1,979 seats
MATERIALS	Stone, marble, and bronze
STYLE	Beaux arts, baroque Revival
DETAILS	Historically known as Opéra de Paris, its opulent setting and a fatal mishap with its grand, 8-ton chandelier, inspired Gaston Leroux's 1910 novel *The Phantom of the Opera*. It was the primary home of the Paris Opera and Paris Opera Ballet until 1989, and houses the Bibliothèque-Musée de l'Opéra National de Paris (Paris Opera Library-Museum).

2. PONT MARIE

CONSTRUCTION	1614–35
ARCHITECT	Christophe Marie
LOCATION	Notre-Dame–Île Saint-Louis
SIZE	302ft (92m) long; 72ft (22m) wide
MATERIALS	Stone
STYLE	Renaissance
DETAILS	One of the oldest bridges in Paris, each of the five arches is different, with niches for sculptures that were never installed.

3. CENTRE POMPIDOU

CONSTRUCTION	1971–77
ARCHITECT	Renzo Piano; Richard Rogers; Gianfranco Franchini; and John Young
LOCATION	Place Georges Pompidou
SIZE	1,111,965ft^2 (103,305m^2) in area; 10 stories
MATERIALS	Steel, glass, and concrete
STYLE	High-tech/structural Expressionism
DETAILS	The industrial aesthetic of the home of the Musée National d'Art Moderne, with its brightly color-coded mechanical systems and glass-enclosed escalator adorning the exterior, is considered a prototype that ushered in a new generation of museums and cultural centers.

4. SACRÉ COEUR

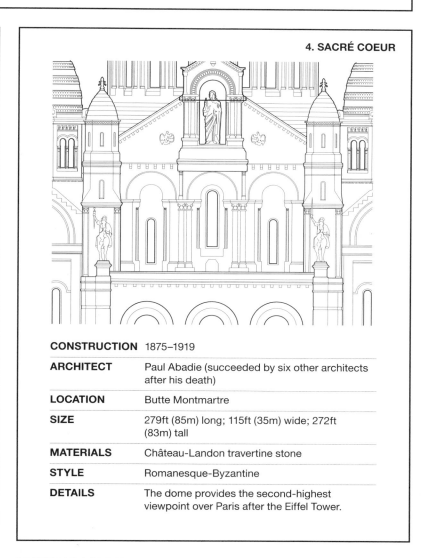

CONSTRUCTION	1875–1919
ARCHITECT	Paul Abadie (succeeded by six other architects after his death)
LOCATION	Butte Montmartre
SIZE	279ft (85m) long; 115ft (35m) wide; 272ft (83m) tall
MATERIALS	Château-Landon travertine stone
STYLE	Romanesque-Byzantine
DETAILS	The dome provides the second-highest viewpoint over Paris after the Eiffel Tower.

5. ARC DE TRIOMPHE DE L'ÉTOILE

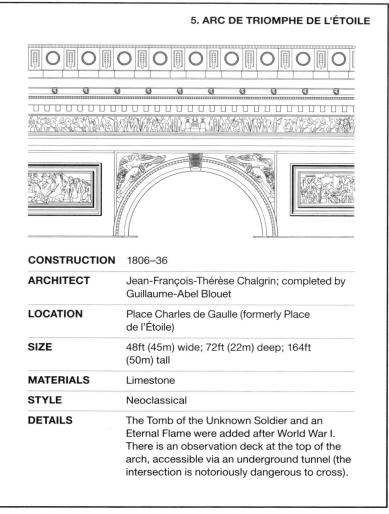

CONSTRUCTION	1806–36
ARCHITECT	Jean-François-Thérèse Chalgrin; completed by Guillaume-Abel Blouet
LOCATION	Place Charles de Gaulle (formerly Place de l'Étoile)
SIZE	48ft (45m) wide; 72ft (22m) deep; 164ft (50m) tall
MATERIALS	Limestone
STYLE	Neoclassical
DETAILS	The Tomb of the Unknown Soldier and an Eternal Flame were added after World War I. There is an observation deck at the top of the arch, accessible via an underground tunnel (the intersection is notoriously dangerous to cross).

NOTRE DAME

CONSTRUCTION	1163–1345
ARCHITECT	Jean de Chelles; Pierre de Montreuil; and Eugène Emmanuel Viollet-le-Duc and Jean-Baptiste-Antoine Lassus (19th-century restoration)
LOCATION	Île de la Cité
SIZE	426ft (130m) long; 157ft (48m) wide; 115ft (35m) tall; twin towers: 223ft (68m) tall
MATERIALS	Stone
STYLE	French Gothic
DETAILS	The cathedral was converted into a food storage warehouse during the French Revolution. In 1991 the most recent restoration was started.

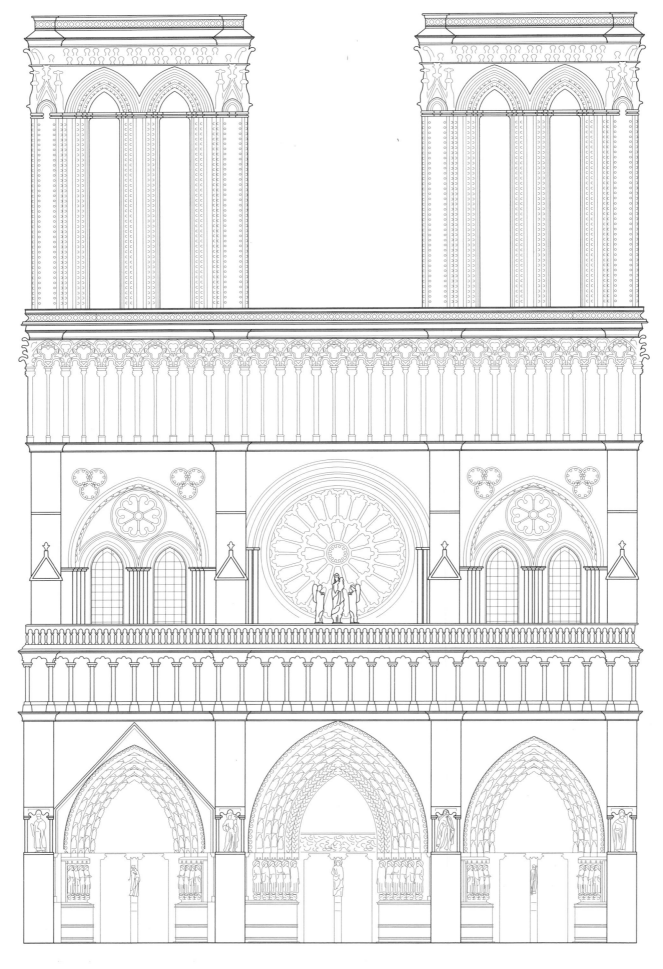

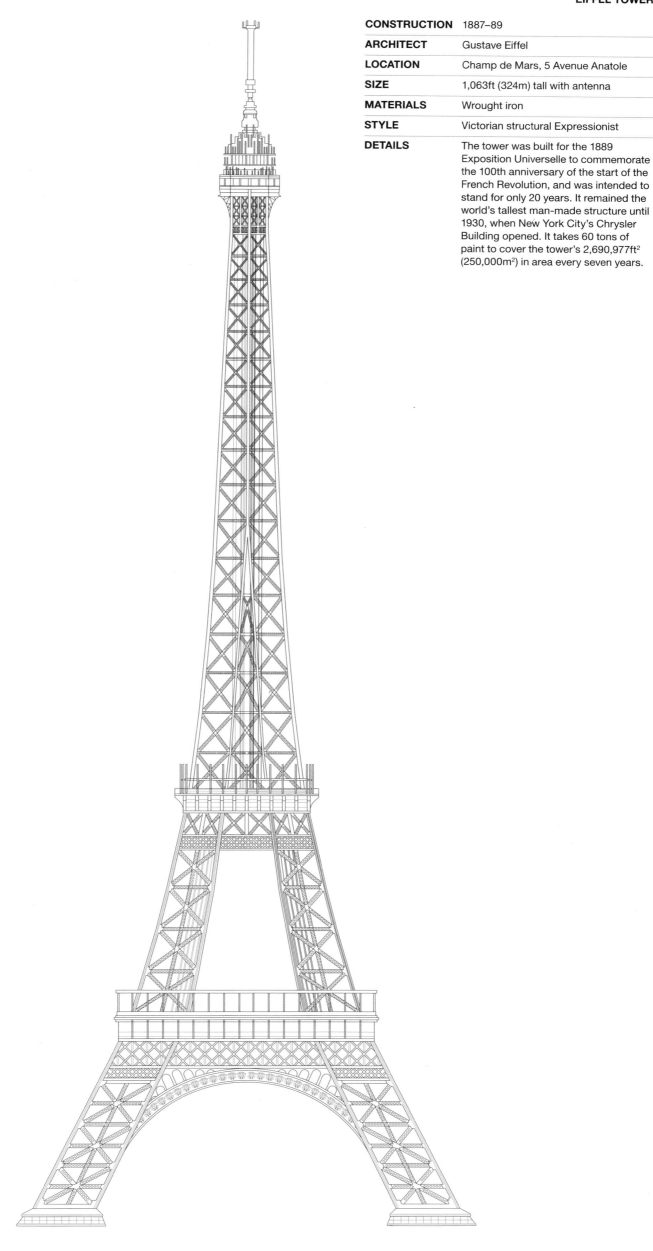

CONSTRUCTION	1887–89
ARCHITECT	Gustave Eiffel
LOCATION	Champ de Mars, 5 Avenue Anatole
SIZE	1,063ft (324m) tall with antenna
MATERIALS	Wrought iron
STYLE	Victorian structural Expressionist
DETAILS	The tower was built for the 1889 Exposition Universelle to commemorate the 100th anniversary of the start of the French Revolution, and was intended to stand for only 20 years. It remained the world's tallest man-made structure until 1930, when New York City's Chrysler Building opened. It takes 60 tons of paint to cover the tower's 2,690,977ft^2 (250,000m^2) in area every seven years.

Amsterdam

1.

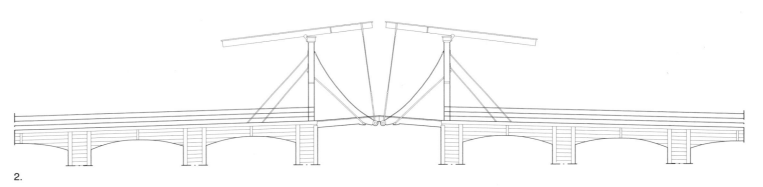

2.

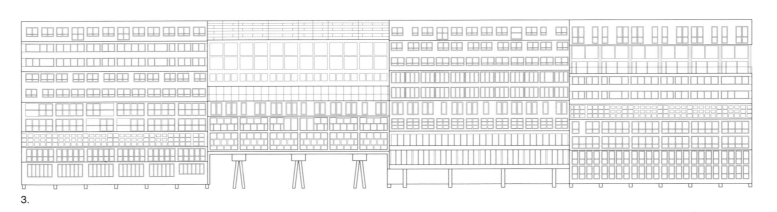

3.

1. CANAL HOUSES
2. MAGERE BRUG
3. SILODAM

Best known for its charming gabled facades and canal houses, Amsterdam boasts a unique urban design that features a pattern of semicircular streets and canals. The city developed in the 13th century as a trade and fishing borough and the dam and canals were built in order to control the Amstel River on its way to the sea. The semicircular canals allowed vessels to enter at one end and exit at the other, without the need to turn around. The medieval houses were built from wood, and only churches and monasteries were built in stone.

Very little architecture is left from this ancient past, but the layout has not changed and the new houses, built in masonry during Amsterdam's Golden Age (thought to fall roughly in the 17th century), are testimony to its subsequent prosperity. The city flourished between the 15th and 16th centuries when it established a colony on Manhattan Island in the city that later became New York.

Houses from this period are a distinctively Dutch mixture of Renaissance, Gothic, and French classical styles. The narrow buildings were designed with workshops below and houses above. Boats had access to them, and most still have a hook to hoist furniture and goods through the windows. The facade is inclined forward, and the top almost always features characteristic Dutch gables.

The city developed southward and made use of its low elevation above sea level to create new developments on reclaimed land. These developments, although more modern in architecture, maintain the traditional plan: narrow facade, at least three stories, with access to a canal.

1. CANAL HOUSES

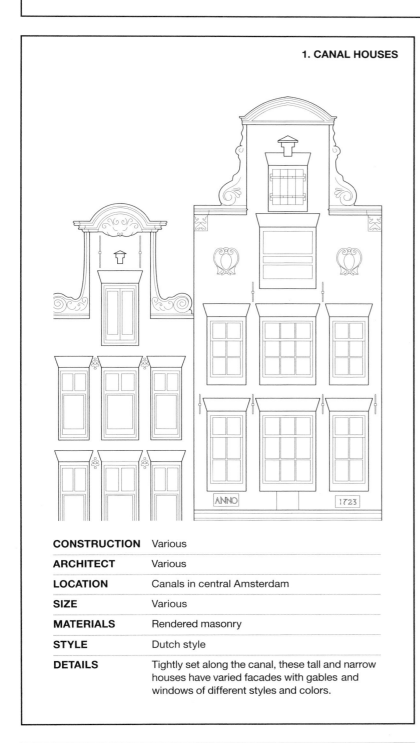

CONSTRUCTION	Various
ARCHITECT	Various
LOCATION	Canals in central Amsterdam
SIZE	Various
MATERIALS	Rendered masonry
STYLE	Dutch style
DETAILS	Tightly set along the canal, these tall and narrow houses have varied facades with gables and windows of different styles and colors.

2. MAGERE BRUG

CONSTRUCTION	Completed 1934
ARCHITECT	Piet Kramer
LOCATION	Amstel River
SIZE	300ft (91m) long
MATERIALS	Wood
STYLE	Typical Dutch double drawbridge
DETAILS	The original pedestrian bridge, built in 1691, was so narrow it was dubbed "Skinny Bridge." While the current bridge is wider, the nickname has stuck. Festooned with more than 1,000 lights at night, it is considered one of the city's most beautiful and romantic sites.

3. SILODAM

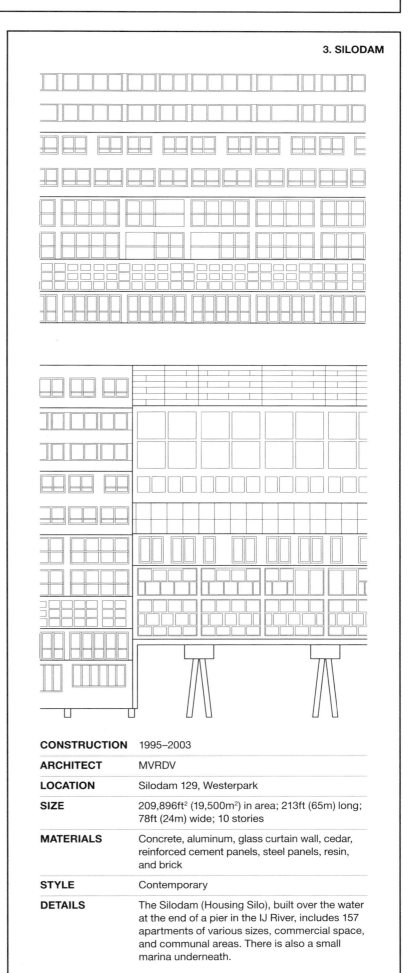

CONSTRUCTION	1995–2003
ARCHITECT	MVRDV
LOCATION	Silodam 129, Westerpark
SIZE	209,896ft² (19,500m²) in area; 213ft (65m) long; 78ft (24m) wide; 10 stories
MATERIALS	Concrete, aluminum, glass curtain wall, cedar, reinforced cement panels, steel panels, resin, and brick
STYLE	Contemporary
DETAILS	The Silodam (Housing Silo), built over the water at the end of a pier in the IJ River, includes 157 apartments of various sizes, commercial space, and communal areas. There is also a small marina underneath.

Florence

3.

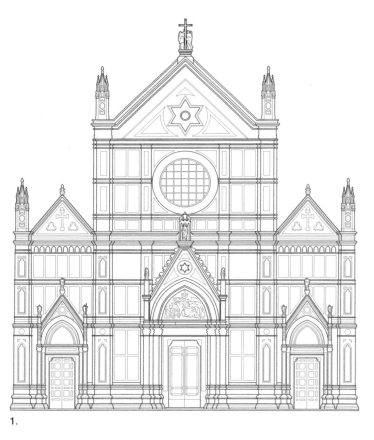

1.

2.

1. SANTA MARIA DEL FIORE (IL DUOMO DI FIRENZE)
2. SANTO SPIRITO
3. BASILICA DI SANTA CROCE

To visit Florence is to dip into the past: Everywhere there are classic buildings, cobbled streets, archways, and narrow alleys. But if you look closely, there is modern design to be found behind each window.

The city is not only the birthplace of the Renaissance but also of the Italian language and of some of the most famous artists, architects, and writers of the period. When viewed from above, the original Roman city's regular grid and the medieval spread that followed are clearly visible. Divided by the Arno River but united by the famous Ponte Vecchio, the city achieved its splendor thanks to the rich merchants' guilds of the late medieval period. In the 13th century these influential businessmen, including the famous Medici family, started a regeneration process in the architecture, art, and culture of the city—and of the world. The city became the birthplace of a new era: the Renaissance.

1. SANTA MARIA DEL FIORE (IL DUOMO DI FIRENZE)

CONSTRUCTION	1296–1436
ARCHITECT	Arnolfo di Cambio and Giotto (bell tower); Andrea Pisano and Lorenzo Ghiberti (baptistery doors); Francesco Talenti and Filippo Brunelleschi (dome); and Emilio De Fabris (19th-century west facade)
LOCATION	Piazza del Duomo
SIZE	502ft (153m) long; 295ft (90m) wide; and 376ft (115m) tall
MATERIALS	Polychrome marble and masonry
STYLE	Italian Gothic, Renaissance, Gothic Revival
DETAILS	Brunelleschi's dome is 171ft (52m) above the floor and spans 144ft (44m). Inside the cupola, restoration of Giorgio Vasari and Federico Zuccari's frescoes began in 1978 and in 1994 it was completed.

2. SANTO SPIRITO

CONSTRUCTION	1444–1488
ARCHITECT	Filippo Brunelleschi; Antonio Manetti; Giovanni da Gaiole; Salvi d'Andrea; and Baccio d'Agnolo (bell tower, 1503)
LOCATION	Piazza Santo Spirito
SIZE	318ft (97m) long; 105ft (32m) wide
MATERIALS	Stone; plaster (exterior); pietra serena sandstone (interior)
STYLE	Renaissance
DETAILS	The 38 chapels contain many important works of art, including a wooden crucifix by Michelangelo, and a copy of his *Pietà*. Because Brunelleschi died before work began on his design for the facade, his successors decided to leave it unadorned.

3. BASILICA DI SANTA CROCE

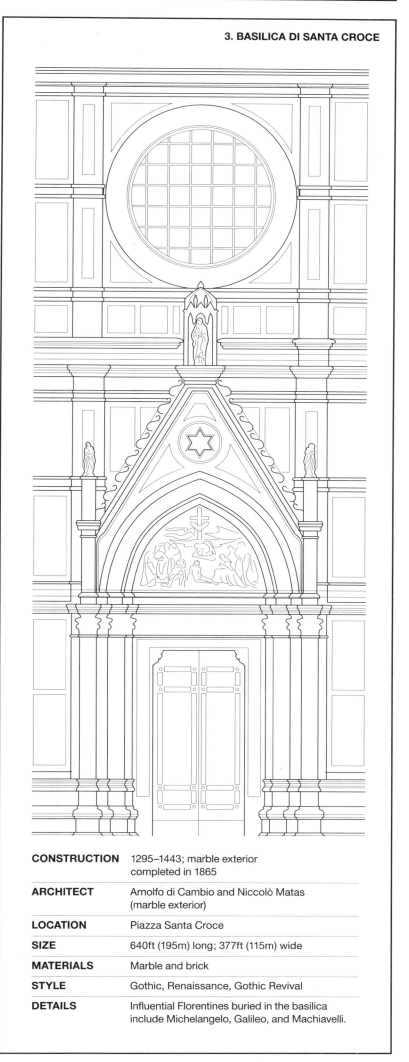

CONSTRUCTION	1295–1443; marble exterior completed in 1865
ARCHITECT	Arnolfo di Cambio and Niccolò Matas (marble exterior)
LOCATION	Piazza Santa Croce
SIZE	640ft (195m) long; 377ft (115m) wide
MATERIALS	Marble and brick
STYLE	Gothic, Renaissance, Gothic Revival
DETAILS	Influential Florentines buried in the basilica include Michelangelo, Galileo, and Machiavelli.

Rome

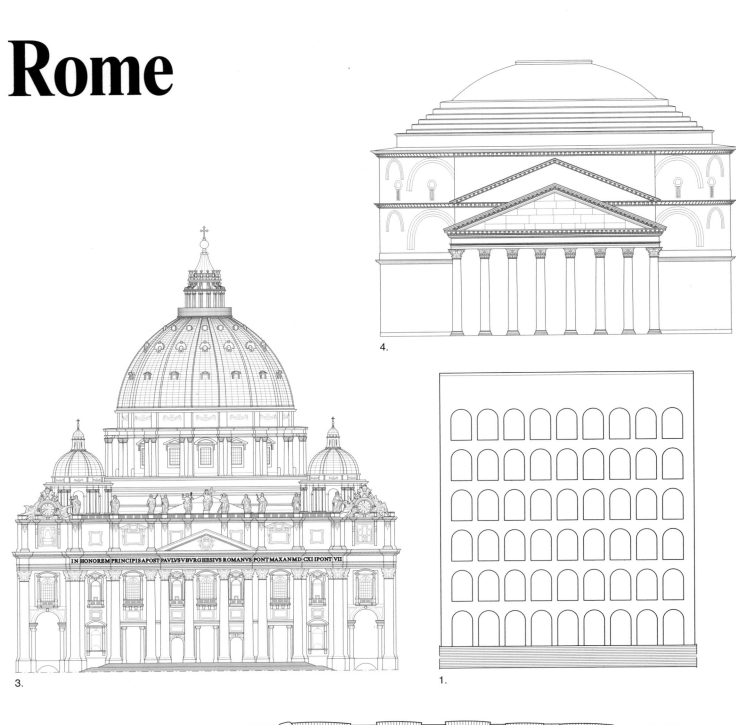

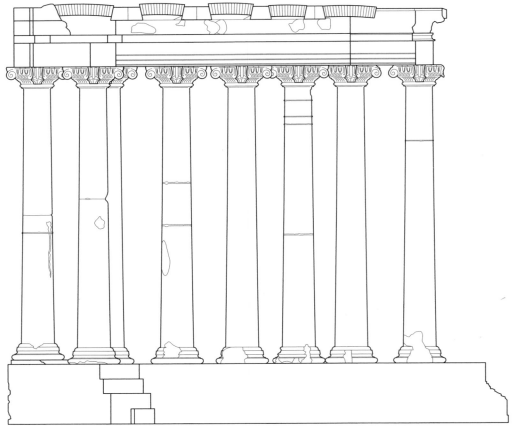

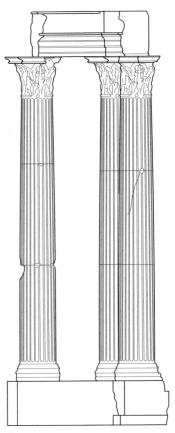

4.

1.

3.

2.

1. PALAZZO DELLA CIVILTÀ ITALIANA
2. FORUM ROMANUM
3. ST. PETER'S BASILICA
4. PANTHEON

Originally set out on seven hills, Rome was the capital of one of the most important empires in the world and is considered to be one of the greatest treasuries of architectural history in the Western world. Layers of history mingle here, ready to be discovered through the city's medieval roads and chaotic traffic.

Within the radius of the ancient city are buildings from every historical period and of most architectural styles. Attempts to demolish buildings that are representative of historic periods have failed and there remain clear examples of structures ravaged by time but still standing.

Italy was the first nation to protect historic buildings, mostly thanks to Rome and the Renaissance, when people of all trades traveled to the city to learn and understand the past by studying these ancient structures. As a result of this protection, modernization has been more difficult, and most developments are located outside the original city center. The Museo dell'Ara Pacis is a notable exception; situated along the Tiber River in the heart of Rome. This travertine, plaster, and glass-clad contemporary museum, designed by Richard Meier & Partners Architects opened in 2006 to much controversy.

1. PALAZZO DELLA CIVILTÀ ITALIANA

CONSTRUCTION	1937–43
ARCHITECT	Giovanni Guerrini; Ernesto Bruno Lapadula; and Mario Romano
LOCATION	Quadrato della Concordia, 5, EUR
SIZE	215278ft^2 (20,000m^2); 6 stories; 216 arches (6 rows of nine floor-height arches on all facades)
MATERIALS	Travertine marble
STYLE	Neoclassical Fascist architecture
DETAILS	Also known as the Colosseo Quadrato (Square Colosseum), it was once the centerpiece of Mussolini's plans for a vast business complex on the outskirts of Rome to celebrate Fascist rule and to host the 1942 World's Fair.

2. FORUM ROMANUM

CONSTRUCTION	6th century BCE–4th century CE
ARCHITECT	Various
LOCATION	Via della Salara Vecchia
SIZE	Adapted in size according to the city population
MATERIALS	Marble and granite
STYLE	Classical
DETAILS	The remains of the Temple of Vespasian and Titus. The temple was used in the festivities to Saturn in December.

3. ST. PETER'S BASILICA

POST·PAVLVS·V·BVRGHESIVS·ROMANVS·PONT

CONSTRUCTION	Completed 1626; dome 1564
ARCHITECT	Donato Bramante, Michelangelo, and others
LOCATION	Piazza San Pietro, 00120 Città del Vaticano
SIZE	623ft (190m) long, 149ft (46m) high nave, 446ft (136m) high dome
MATERIALS	Brick, limestone, marble
STYLE	Classical
DETAILS	The apostle St. Peter, the first Pope, is said to be buried here.

4. PANTHEON

CONSTRUCTION	118–125
ARCHITECT	Under the supervision of Emperor Hadrian
LOCATION	Piazza della Rotonda
SIZE	141ft (43m) height and diameter
MATERIALS	Brick, Roman concrete, marble, granite
STYLE	Classical
DETAILS	This is the best-preserved and one of the most fascinating buildings in Rome. The interior space was designed as a perfect sphere and the dome was the biggest in the world until Santa Maria del Fiore in Florence was built. It is also the only dome to be constructed in non-reinforced concrete.

Copenhagen

3.

5.

2.

4.

1.

1. NYHAVN (NEW HARBOR) 2. DANMARKS NATIONALBANK
3. GRUNDTVIG'S CHURCH 4. CHURCH OF OUR SAVIOR
5. THE MARBLE CHURCH (FREDERIKS KIRKE)

Copenhagen is acclaimed for an architectural history that displays a commitment to ensuring buildings are beautiful as well as sustainable. Every neighborhood has a strong, vibrant color and displays a variety of architectural styles.

The city dates back to an 11th-century Viking fishing village, on the east of the island. Under the protection of Archbishop Absalon, the city prospered thanks to the fishing industry and the harbor that allowed it to emerge as a trading center. It was not until the late 15th century that it became the capital of Denmark and the largest city in Scandinavia. The biggest architectural development came in the 17th century when the architect-king Christian IV developed the merchant village Christianshavn, now a neighborhood in modern Copenhagen.

As with many port cities, the industrial revolution brought further development and growth and by the 1900s, Denmark had adopted the simple and minimalist Scandinavian style, both in its architecture and in furniture and design.

1. NYHAVN (NEW HARBOR)

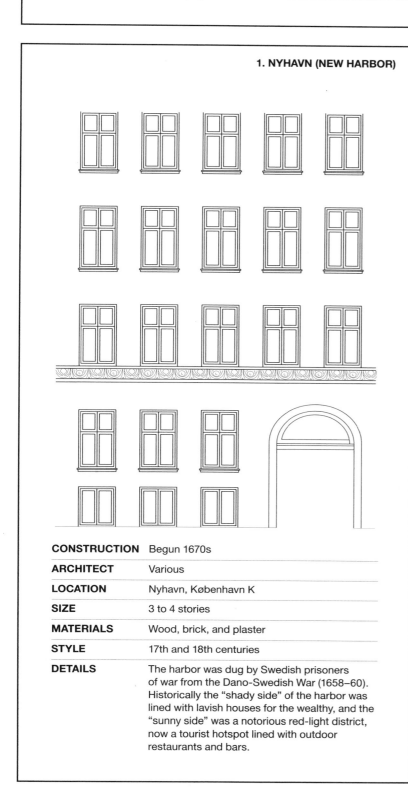

CONSTRUCTION	Begun 1670s
ARCHITECT	Various
LOCATION	Nyhavn, København K
SIZE	3 to 4 stories
MATERIALS	Wood, brick, and plaster
STYLE	17th and 18th centuries
DETAILS	The harbor was dug by Swedish prisoners of war from the Dano-Swedish War (1658–60). Historically the "shady side" of the harbor was lined with lavish houses for the wealthy, and the "sunny side" was a notorious red-light district, now a tourist hotspot lined with outdoor restaurants and bars.

2. DANMARKS NATIONALBANK

CONSTRUCTION	1965–78
ARCHITECT	Arne Jacobsen in collaboration with Hans Dissing and Otto Weitling
LOCATION	Havnegade 5
SIZE	516,668ft² (48,000m²) in area
MATERIALS	Unhewn stone, marble, steel, and glass
STYLE	Modernist
DETAILS	Considered one of Jacobsen's masterpieces, in 2009 the building listed as a historical site. Many of the interior fixtures and furnishings were also designed by the architect. Among his many notable buildings in the city is the SAS Royal Hotel Copenhagen, for which he designed the famous Egg Chair in 1958.

3. GRUNDTVIG'S CHURCH

CONSTRUCTION	1921–40
ARCHITECT	Peder Vilhelm Jensen-Klint; completed by Jensen-Klint's son, Kaare Klint, and grandson Esben Klint
LOCATION	På Bjerget 14B, Bispebjerg
SIZE	249ft (76m) long; 115ft (35m) wide; 161ft (49m) tall
MATERIALS	Yellow brick
STYLE	Expressionism with Gothic influence
DETAILS	It took 6 million yellow bricks, handmade locally, to build the church.

4. CHURCH OF OUR SAVIOR

CONSTRUCTION	1682–96; spire completed in 1752
ARCHITECT	Lambert van Haven (church); Lauritz de Thurah (spire)
LOCATION	Sankt Annæ Gade 29, Christianshavn
SIZE	295ft (90m) tall
MATERIALS	Yellow and red bricks, a granite foundation, and a black-glazed tile roof. The black spire has golden detail.
STYLE	Baroque
DETAILS	The 400 steps leading to the top of the corkscrew-shaped, black with gilded-iron, spire include a 150-step external staircase that is not for the faint of heart.

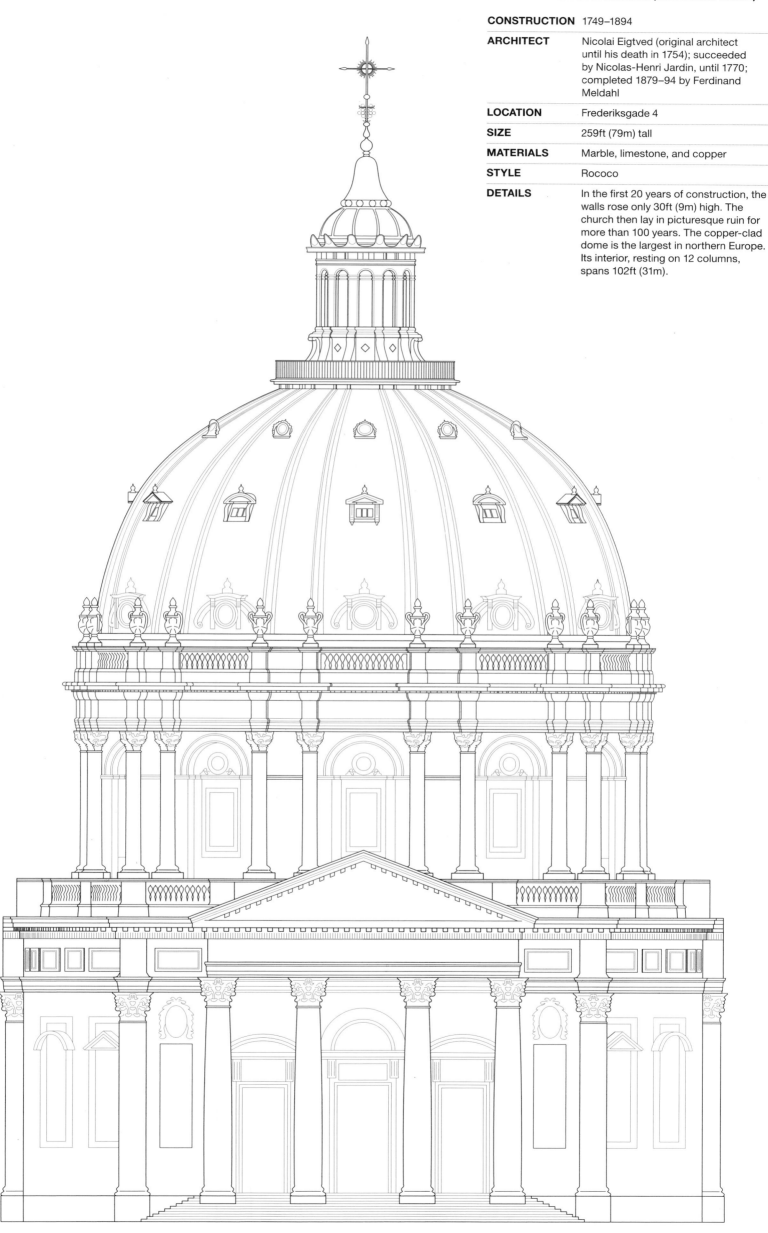

5. THE MARBLE CHURCH (FREDERIKS KIRKE)

CONSTRUCTION	1749–1894
ARCHITECT	Nicolai Eigtved (original architect until his death in 1754); succeeded by Nicolas-Henri Jardin, until 1770; completed 1879–94 by Ferdinand Meldahl
LOCATION	Frederiksgade 4
SIZE	259ft (79m) tall
MATERIALS	Marble, limestone, and copper
STYLE	Rococo
DETAILS	In the first 20 years of construction, the walls rose only 30ft (9m) high. The church then lay in picturesque ruin for more than 100 years. The copper-clad dome is the largest in northern Europe. Its interior, resting on 12 columns, spans 102ft (31m).

Berlin

1. BRANDENBURG GATE
2. NEW NATIONAL GALLERY (NEUE NATIONALGALERIE)
3. BERLIN TELEVISION TOWER (BERLINER FERNSEHTURM)
4. AM KUPFERGRABEN 10 5. BERLIN VICTORY COLUMN

Berlin's history dates back to the 13th century, but it had an architecturally uneventful start until Friedrich I crowned himself as the Prussian king in 1701 and established his capital in Berlin. The walls were extended, the palace built, and schools and hospitals founded. By the end of the century the walled city had become an economic center of culture and art. The Brandenburg Gate was built during this period, followed by several other important structures.

By the late 1800s Berlin was the capital of the German Reich. After World War II the city fell into the control of the Allies, who divided it into four sectors: the east under Soviet control as the capital of East Germany; and the west under British, American, and French control. In 1961 a wall was built to divide the city in half and for 30 years the city developed in two architecturally different ways: the west with contemporary architecture such as the New National Gallery and the east with huge socialist housing estates. Since the 1990s the German capital has been moved from Bonn back to Berlin and the city has been rebuilding itself as a contemporary hub of culture and business.

1. BRANDENBURG GATE

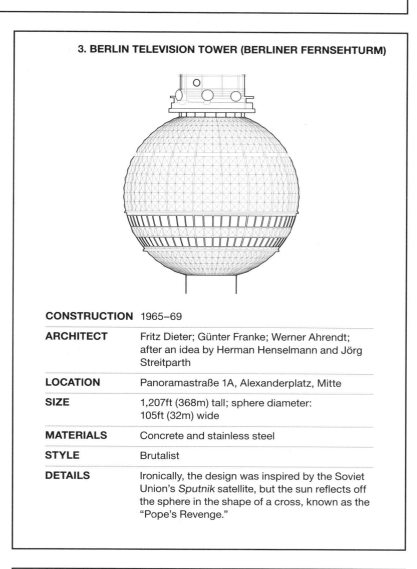

CONSTRUCTION	1788–91
ARCHITECT	Carl Gotthard Langhans; Johann Gottfried Schadow (sculptor)
LOCATION	Pariser Platz
SIZE	213ft (65m) wide; 36ft (11m) deep; 66ft (20m) tall (not including the sculpture)
MATERIALS	Sandstone and bronze
STYLE	Neoclassical
DETAILS	In 1806, Napoléon took the bronze sculpture of the Roman goddess of victory in a horse-drawn chariot, a quadriga, atop the gate to Paris; it was returned in 1814 after his defeat.

2. NEW NATIONAL GALLERY (NEUE NATIONALGALERIE)

CONSTRUCTION	1962–68
ARCHITECT	Ludwig Mies van der Rohe
LOCATION	Potsdamer Strasse 50, Kulturforum
SIZE	Pavilion: 27,556ft² (2,560m²) in area; roof: 45,198ft² (4,199m²) in area; lower level: 107,639ft² (10,000m²) in area
MATERIALS	Glass, steel, granite, and aluminum
STYLE	Modernist
DETAILS	Mies's final masterpiece, the glass pavilion with its dramatic cantilevered roof was based on a never-realized design for the Bacardi rum company's headquarters in Cuba.

3. BERLIN TELEVISION TOWER (BERLINER FERNSEHTURM)

CONSTRUCTION	1965–69
ARCHITECT	Fritz Dieter; Günter Franke; Werner Ahrendt; after an idea by Herman Henselmann and Jörg Streitparth
LOCATION	Panoramastraße 1A, Alexanderplatz, Mitte
SIZE	1,207ft (368m) tall; sphere diameter: 105ft (32m) wide
MATERIALS	Concrete and stainless steel
STYLE	Brutalist
DETAILS	Ironically, the design was inspired by the Soviet Union's *Sputnik* satellite, but the sun reflects off the sphere in the shape of a cross, known as the "Pope's Revenge."

4. AM KUPFERGRABEN 10

CONSTRUCTION	2003–07
ARCHITECT	David Chipperfield Architects
LOCATION	Am Kupfergraben 10
SIZE	21,528ft² (2,000m²) in area
MATERIALS	Brick, concrete, glass, and wood
STYLE	Contemporary
DETAILS	The art gallery overlooking Museum Island occupies the footprint of a building destroyed in World War II. The facades incorporate salvaged bricks from the original building. Until 2016 it was home to the Contemporary Fine Arts–Mitte gallery.

5. BERLIN VICTORY COLUMN (SIEGESSÄULE)

CONSTRUCTION	1864–73
ARCHITECT	Heinrich Strack (column); Friedrich Drake (bronze sculpture); and Anton von Werner (mosaics)
LOCATION	Große Stern (Great Star) plaza
SIZE	219.8ft (67m) high
MATERIALS	Red granite, sandstone, and bronze
STYLE	Neoclassical
DETAILS	Affectionately referred to as "Golden Lizzie" by Berliners, the column was originally situated opposite the Reichstag building on Platz der Republik, known as Königsplatz (Square of the King) at the time. In 1939 it was removed to its current location by the Nazis.

KAISER WILHELM MEMORIAL CHURCH (GEDÄCHTNISKIRCHE)

CONSTRUCTION	1891–95
ARCHITECT	Franz Schwechten
LOCATION	Breitscheidplatz
SIZE	230ft (70m) tall; originally 370ft (113m) tall
MATERIALS	Stone
STYLE	Romanesque revival
DETAILS	All but the west tower was destroyed in World War II. It was going to be demolished and replaced in 1956, but citizens saw the ruin as an anti-war memorial. A Modernist church, designed by Egon Eiermann, was completed in 1963 adjacent to the historic tower, which now houses the memorial hall.

Johannesburg

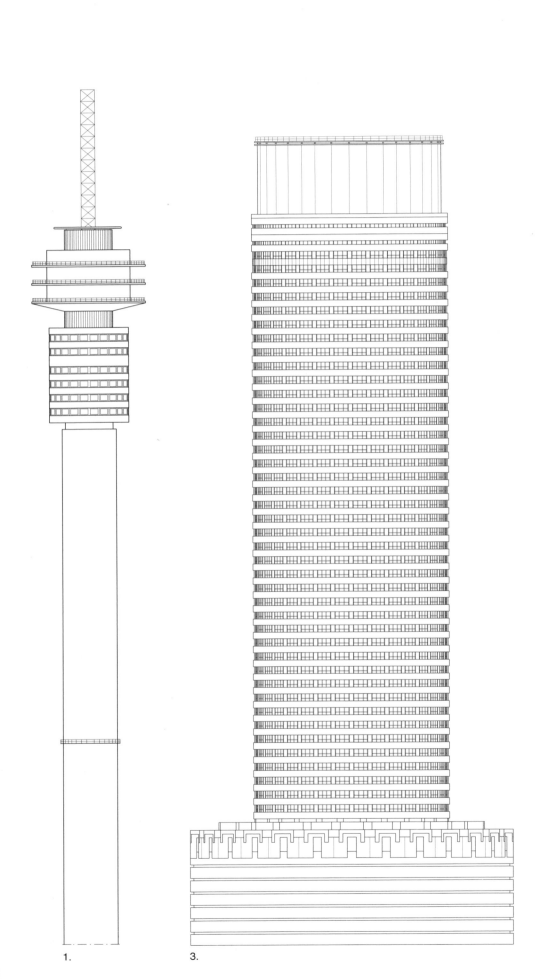

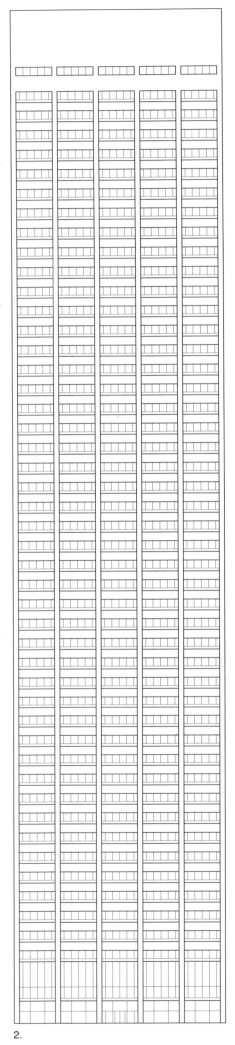

1.

3.

2.

1. HILLBROW TOWER
2. CARLTON CENTRE
3. PONTE CITY APARTMENTS

Today Johannesburg is the largest and most important city in South Africa, and a commercial center for all of Africa. This contemporary city is filled with character and is also a city of contrast between locals and immigrant job seekers, rich and poor, global corporations and small local businesses.

The city developed due to the discovery of gold in the late 1800s, when an ever-growing community of miners settled in squalid conditions. A health committee was given authority over the city in 1889, and it evolved into a neat, square grid. The city grew notably in the 1960s and 70s with the building of several skyscrapers, including the Carlton Centre and Ponte City. By the 1980s the city fell into decline with numerous riots and political instability. The Ponte City residential tower became the most famous slum in the world. However, in the 1990s the city started a regeneration process that has led, especially in the last decade, to its becoming the most advanced commercial city in South Africa.

1. HILLBROW TOWER

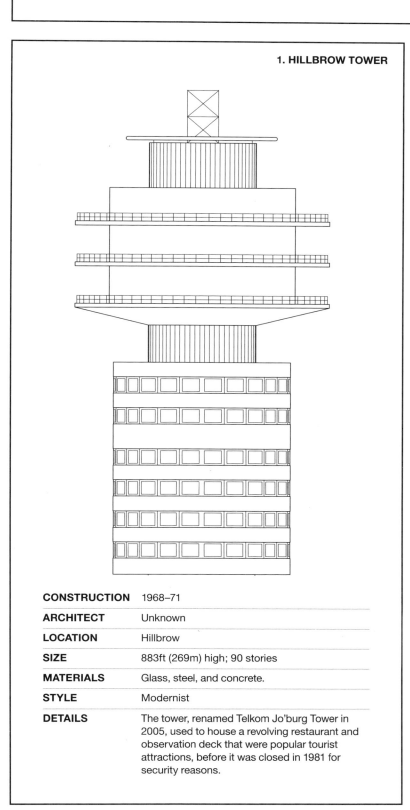

CONSTRUCTION	1968–71
ARCHITECT	Unknown
LOCATION	Hillbrow
SIZE	883ft (269m) high; 90 stories
MATERIALS	Glass, steel, and concrete.
STYLE	Modernist
DETAILS	The tower, renamed Telkom Jo'burg Tower in 2005, used to house a revolving restaurant and observation deck that were popular tourist attractions, before it was closed in 1981 for security reasons.

2. CARLTON CENTRE

CONSTRUCTION	1967–73
ARCHITECT	Skidmore, Owings & Merrill (SOM); and W. Rhodes-Harrison Hoffe and Partners
LOCATION	150 Commissioner Street
SIZE	811,110ft^2 (75,355m^2) in area; 732ft (223m) tall; 50 stories
MATERIALS	Concrete, granite, steel, and glass
STYLE	Brutalist
DETAILS	Housing offices and a retail center, this is currently the tallest building in Africa, with an observation deck on the 50th floor called the "Top of Africa."

3. PONTE CITY APARTMENTS

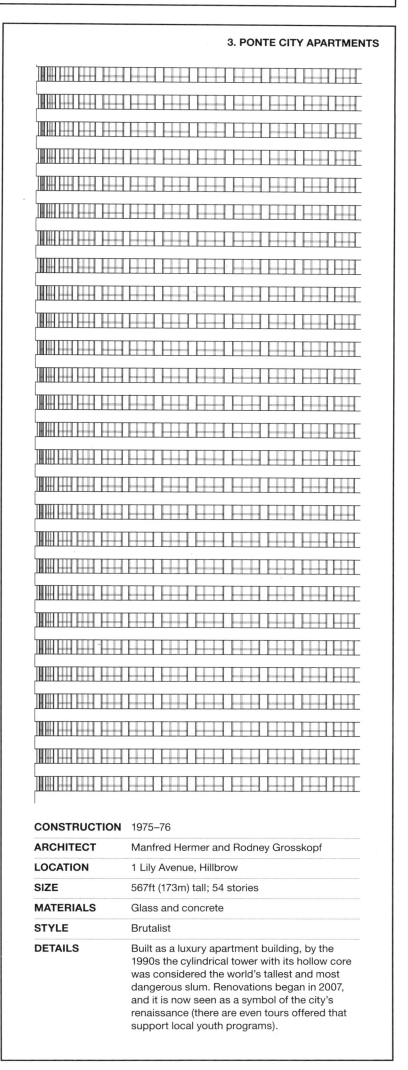

CONSTRUCTION	1975–76
ARCHITECT	Manfred Hermer and Rodney Grosskopf
LOCATION	1 Lily Avenue, Hillbrow
SIZE	567ft (173m) tall; 54 stories
MATERIALS	Glass and concrete
STYLE	Brutalist
DETAILS	Built as a luxury apartment building, by the 1990s the cylindrical tower with its hollow core was considered the world's tallest and most dangerous slum. Renovations began in 2007, and it is now seen as a symbol of the city's renaissance (there are even tours offered that support local youth programs).

Stockholm

1.

2.

3.

4.

5.

1. KAKNÄSTORNET 2. STOCKHOLM CITY HALL
3. STOCKHOLM PUBLIC LIBRARY
4. STOCKHOLM CONCERT HALL
(KONSERTHUSET STOCKHOLM)
5. STORTORGET (GREAT SQUARE)

In the 13th century Stockholm was a fortified town that functioned as a trade port with Europe, and Germany in particular. The influence of German architecture can be seen in areas such as Stortorget (Great Square) in the Gamla Stan (Old Town), with their colorful facades and gabled roofs.

As the city developed there was a need for more space, and it started connecting with nearby islands. The Stockholm canals are channels between islands that are connected by bridges. These characteristics give the city a unique identity, since each island has a regular structure within it but is different from the next. The city hall, for example, located at the corner of one island, can be seen from the Old Town as the entrance to the city.

As with most industrial cities in the western world, manufacturing and heavy labor have moved out, leaving behind a prosperous city. It is clear that Stockholm has given great importance to culture, especially to dance and music. The city hosts events all year round with 1,500 artists in residence and more venues than most cities.

4. STOCKHOLM CONCERT HALL (KONSERTHUSET STOCKHOLM)

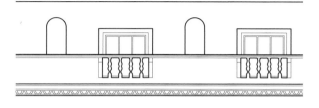

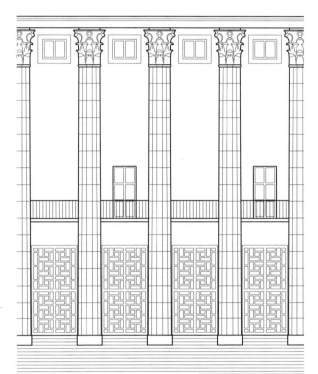

CONSTRUCTION	1923–26
ARCHITECT	Ivar Tengbom
LOCATION	Hötorget 8
SIZE	198ft (60m) long; 164ft (50m) wide; 6 stories; 2 theaters sit 1,600 and 450
MATERIALS	Blue stucco and gray granite
STYLE	Neoclassical
DETAILS	The strikingly blue-colored building is the home of the Royal Stockholm Philharmonic Orchestra. It also hosts concerts and awards ceremonies, including the Nobel Prize Award Ceremony.

1. KAKNÄSTORNET

CONSTRUCTION	1964–67
ARCHITECT	Hans Borgström, Bengt Lindroos, Sven Olof Asplund (engineer)
LOCATION	Mörka Kroken 28-30, Ladugårdsgärdet Park
SIZE	509ft (155m) tall, 558ft (170m), including the mast
MATERIALS	Concrete and glass
STYLE	Brutalist
DETAILS	Stockholm's second-tallest building houses a restaurant, bar, and observation deck. The copper, nickel, and enamel relief set in the concrete symbolizes radio and television waves.

3. STOCKHOLM PUBLIC LIBRARY

CONSTRUCTION	1924–28
ARCHITECT	Gunnar Asplund
LOCATION	Sveavägen 73
SIZE	161ft (49m) long; 160ft (49m) wide; 103ft (31m) tall; 4 stories
MATERIALS	Brick and orange plaster
STYLE	Nordic Classicism and Swedish Grace
DETAILS	In early sketches, the library had a traditional classicist design with a cupola but it was replaced with a monumental cylindrical form jutting out of a square base in the final design. A restoration and expansion by British firm Caruso St. John, in collaboration with local firm Scheiwiller Svensson Arkitektkontor, should be completed by 2019.

2. STOCKHOLM CITY HALL

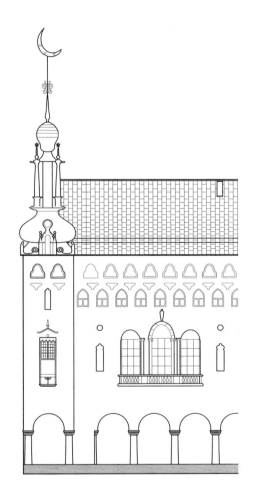

CONSTRUCTION	1911–23
ARCHITECT	Ragnar Östberg
LOCATION	Hantverkargatan 1, Kungsholmen
SIZE	348ft (106m) tall (tower)
MATERIALS	Dark red brick
STYLE	National Romantic
DETAILS	Blå Hallen (Blue Hall) hosts the annual Nobel Banquet. It was named for what was to have been a blue interior, but the architect decided the red brick should remain exposed.

5. STORTORGET (GREAT SQUARE)

CONSTRUCTION	13th to 17th centuries
ARCHITECT	Various
LOCATION	Gamla Stan (Old Town)
SIZE	3 to 5 stories
MATERIALS	Brick, wood, and plaster
STYLE	Predominantly Nordic Renaissance
DETAILS	Stockholm's oldest square is located in Gamla Stan, or Old Town, where the city was founded in 1252.

Moscow

5.

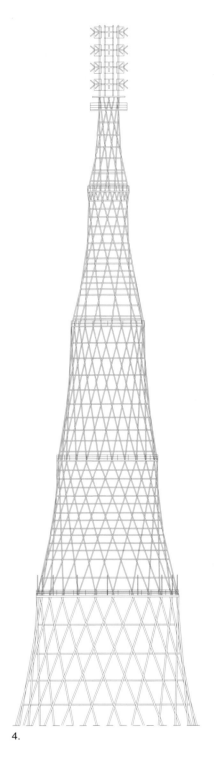

4.

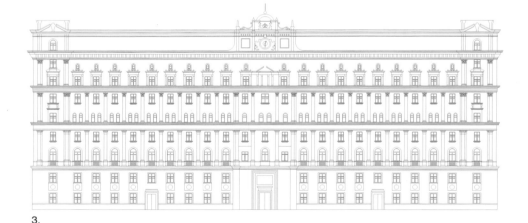

3.

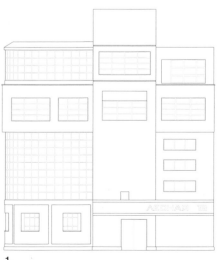

1.

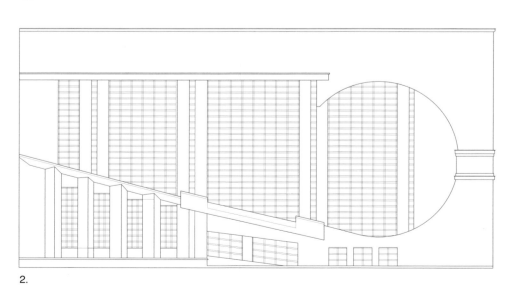

2.

1. ZUEV WORKERS' CLUB 2. INTOURIST GARAGE
3. LUBYANKA BUILDING
4. SHUKHOV TOWER
5. SAINT BASIL'S CATHEDRAL

The city of Moscow developed from a walled city, the Kremlin, in the 12th century to become the capital of Russia in the 15th century. It is a triangular, fortified area that underwent many transformations, fires, moats, and rebuilds. The Red Square, today the center of the city, was originally on the poorer outskirts. As the city developed, it grew in concentric circles and radial streets out from the Kremlin.

The older buildings, such as the towers on the Kremlin walls or the famous cathedral of St. Basil with its colorful Russian–Byzantine domes, are at the heart of the city. The classical and baroque buildings are on the first ring. The growth slowed down during the 18th century due to the move of the capital to St. Petersburg, but it did not stop altogether. The modern movement of the 20th century arrived in Russia and mixed with previous styles to become the Russian constructivism seen in buildings like the Zuev Workers' Club and the Intourist Garage. These examples can be seen outside the third ring of the city, near the final stage of housing, the prefabricated apartment blocks, of the Communist era.

1. ZUEV WORKERS' CLUB

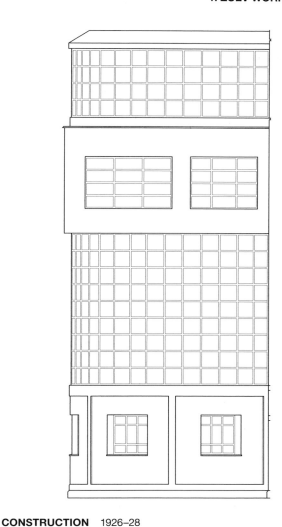

CONSTRUCTION	1926–28
ARCHITECT	Ilya Golosov
LOCATION	18 Lesnaya Ulitsa
SIZE	Includes an 850-seat auditorium*
MATERIALS	Concrete and glass
STYLE	Constructivist
DETAILS	Built as a clubhouse and cultural center for the Union of Communal Services members, the building is an iconic work of Soviet avant-garde architecture, combining strong rectilinear forms with a dramatic glass-enclosed cylindrical corner facade housing an interior staircase. Much of the rest of the glazing was bricked over and balconies removed in the 1970s. It still operates as a cultural center, including a children's theater.

2. INTOURIST GARAGE

CONSTRUCTION	1933–36
ARCHITECT	Konstantin Melnikov with V. I. Kurochkin
LOCATION	33 Sushchevsky Val
SIZE	Approx. 5 stories
MATERIALS	Concrete
STYLE	Constructivist
DETAILS	One of several of Melnikov's avant-garde garages, today, only the geometric facade remains.

3. LUBYANKA BUILDING

CONSTRUCTION	Completed in 1898; extended in 1947 and 1983
ARCHITECT	Alexander V. Ivanov (designer, 1898); expanded by Aleksey Shchusev from 1940 to 1947
LOCATION	Lubyanka Square, Meshchansky District
SIZE	Approx. 6 stories
MATERIALS	Yellow brick, granite, and sandstone
STYLE	Baroque revival
DETAILS	Originally built in 1898 for the All-Russia Insurance Company, this massive building served as KGB headquarters, and included the infamous Lubyanka prison from 1954 until the fall of the Soviet Union in 1991. It currently houses the KGB's successor, the Federal Security Service (FSB). Tours and a small museum are available by appointment.

4. SHUKHOV TOWER

CONSTRUCTION	1920–22
ARCHITECT	Vladimir Shukhov
LOCATION	Shabolovka Street 8
SIZE	525ft (160m) tall
MATERIALS	Steel
STYLE	Constructivist
DETAILS	Also known as the Shabolovka Radio Tower, the hyperboloid design was originally meant to be twice as tall, but steel was in short supply during the Russian Civil War. In 2014 protests led to scrapping plans to relocate it, and it was added to the 2016 World Monuments Watch in hopes of it getting a much-needed restoration.

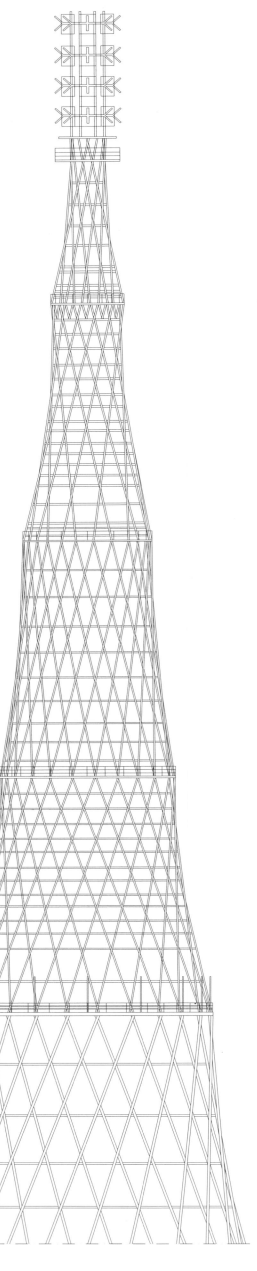

CONSTRUCTION	1555–61
ARCHITECT	Disputed—Postnik Yakovlev and Ivan Barma; or Ivan Yakovlevich Barma; or brothers Barma and Postnik Yakovlev; or Barma may have been Yakovlev's assistant
LOCATION	Red Square
SIZE	266ft (81m) tall
MATERIALS	Wood, stone, brick, and gold
STYLE	Russian vernacular Renaissance and Byzantine
DETAILS	The cathedral was originally commissioned by Ivan the Terrible and it was between the 1680s and 1848 that the remarkable colors of the cathedral and its nine surrounding churches were added. In 1923 a young Soviet Union converted the cathedral into a museum of architecture and history, and in 1929 it became a branch of the State Historical Museum. The cathedral now holds occassional church services.

Dubai

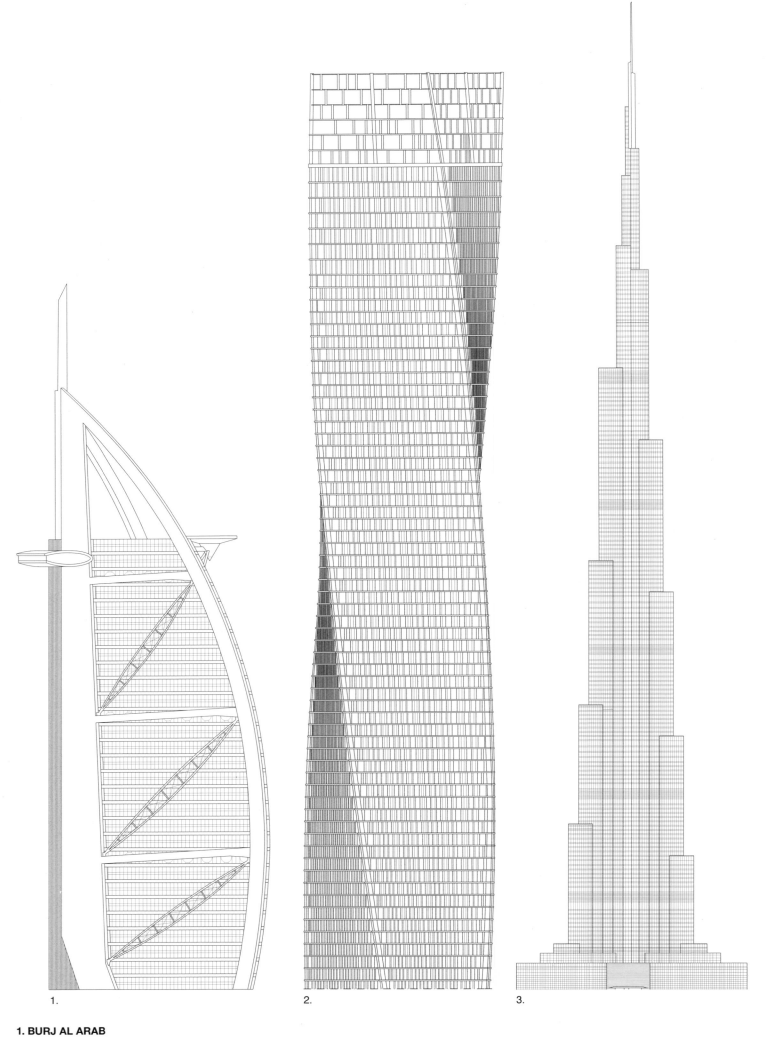

1.

2.

3.

1. BURJ AL ARAB
2. CAYAN TOWER
3. BURJ KHALIFA

Archaeological records date Dubai as a caravan post as far back as the Iron Age. It remained so until the 1800s when the Bani Yas tribe settled in the creek, which created a natural harbor that was ideal for stopover trading. In 1883 the city developed and became an independent state. Its wealth came from the pearling industry, and the city flourished with the biggest souk (market) in the region.

In the 1950s the creek was dredged, and a bigger, better harbor was created, which enhanced the city's trade position and economy. Today's Dubai owes its prosperity to the discovery of oil in the 1960s. Since then the city has become a hub for technology, infrastructure, and architecture. The Burj Khalifa claims to be the first seven-star hotel and the tallest building in the world.

The city is a long strip by the sea that has been expanding over the seabed rather than on land. With new technology, the newly created islands do not need to follow a geological contour, a structural restriction, or an urban grid.

1. BURJ AL ARAB

CONSTRUCTION	1994–99
ARCHITECT	Tom Wright of Atkins (design); KCA International (interior)
LOCATION	Jumeirah Beach Road
SIZE	2,152,782ft² (120,000m²) in area; 1,053ft (321m) tall; 56 stories; 648ft (197.5m) highest floor
MATERIALS	Steel, concrete, and glass
STYLE	Contemporary exterior and opulent interior
DETAILS	This super-luxury hotel shaped like a Persian Gulf dhow (sailboat) includes a soaring atrium (597ft/182m high) and a helipad attached to the exterior, 695ft (212m) above the sea.

2. CAYAN TOWER

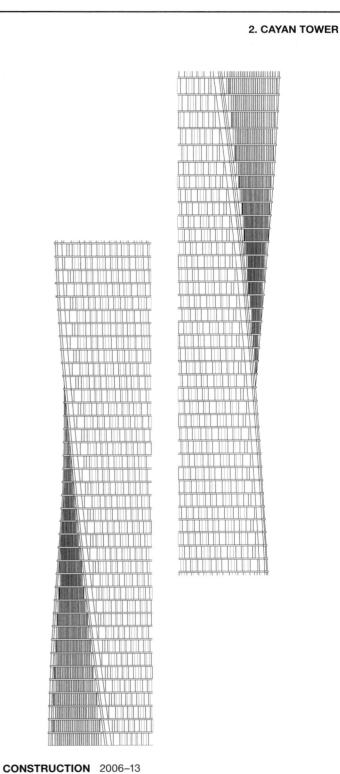

CONSTRUCTION	2006–13
ARCHITECT	Skidmore, Owings & Merrill (SOM) with Khatib & Alami
LOCATION	Al Sufouh Road, Dubai Marina
SIZE	1,194,794ft² (111,000m²) in area; 1,005ft (306m) tall; 75 stories
MATERIALS	Glass, steel, and concrete
STYLE	Contemporary
DETAILS	Also known as the Infinity Tower, this 495-unit luxury residential building forms an eye-catching helix. Each floor is identical, but twists 1.2 degrees in relation to the floor below, altogether completing a 90-degree twist.

3. BURJ KHALIFA

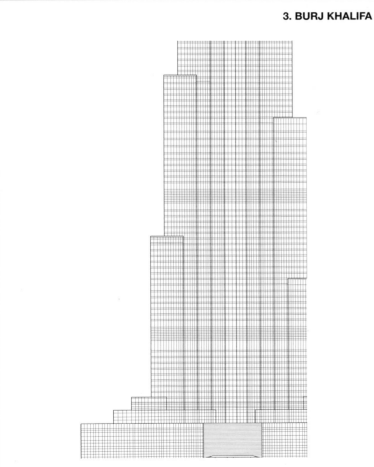

CONSTRUCTION	2004–10
ARCHITECT	Skidmore, Owings & Merrill (SOM), Adrian Smith (design), William F. Baker (structural engineer)
LOCATION	1 Sheikh Mohammed bin Rashid Boulevard
SIZE	3,331,140ft² (309,473m²) in area; 2,717ft (828m) tall; 163 stories; interior space: 2,000,000ft² (185,800m²) in area
MATERIALS	Steel, concrete, glass, and aluminum
STYLE	Contemporary
DETAILS	The design for the tallest building in the world (for the time being) is based on the *Hymenocallis* flower. Observation decks on the 124th and 148th floors are among the world's highest.

Golden Triangle (Delhi, Agra, and Jaipur)

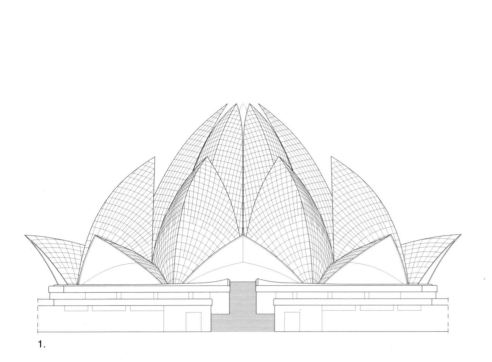

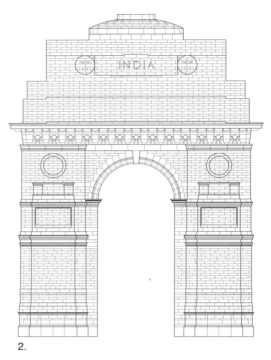

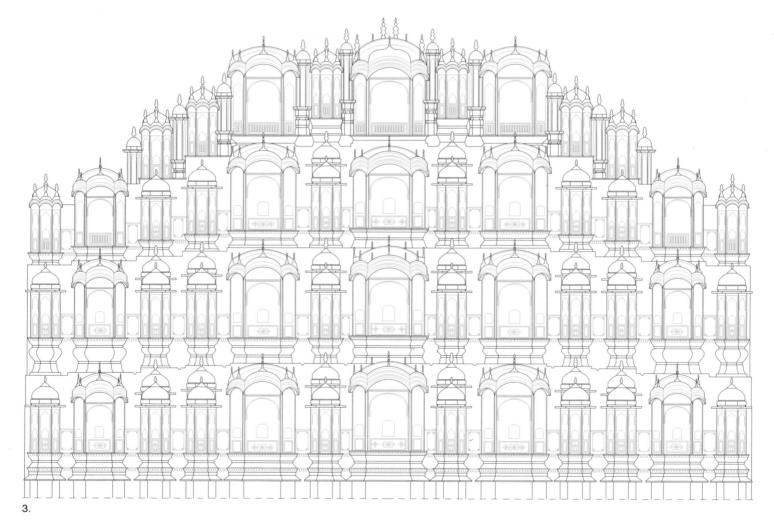

1. LOTUS TEMPLE
2. INDIA GATE
3. HAWA MAHAL

The Golden Triangle is not a city but a triangular journey between three cities in India: Delhi, Agra, and Jaipur. The splendor of the buildings within these cities gives it the prefix of "Golden." A portion of north India is one of the oldest civilizations in the world, if not the oldest. Delhi, its capital, and Agra are mentioned in the Sanskrit epic, the *Mahabharata*. However, it was the era of the Moguls that brought northern India to its most spectacular period of development, from the Taj Mahal in Agra to the Red Fort in Old Delhi. Both cities suffered wars and invasions and most recently a long period of British colonial rule, so it was not until 1947 that India became independent. Agra and Delhi have both been capitals in one period or another, and their architecture is a showcase of their importance.

Jaipur has a different story: It was planned and designed in the 1700s. The plan consisted of nine squares divided by big avenues with trees. Each of these squares was a neighborhood with a square grid within it. The palace quarter, with the Hawa Mahal at the center, occupied two squares. The city's characteristic pink color was added in 1818 to honor the visit of the Prince of Wales. The pink was retained since it reflected the sunshine without the glare, helping to withstand the blistering desert heat.

1. LOTUS TEMPLE

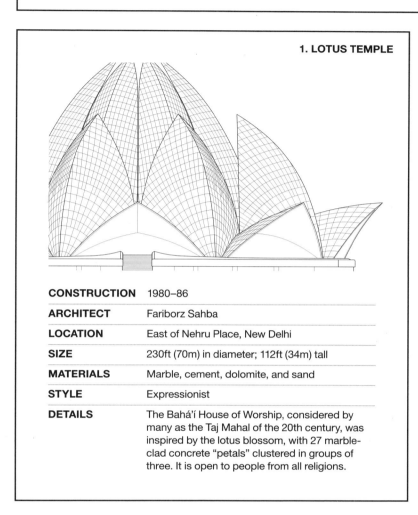

CONSTRUCTION	1980–86
ARCHITECT	Fariborz Sahba
LOCATION	East of Nehru Place, New Delhi
SIZE	230ft (70m) in diameter; 112ft (34m) tall
MATERIALS	Marble, cement, dolomite, and sand
STYLE	Expressionist
DETAILS	The Bahá'í House of Worship, considered by many as the Taj Mahal of the 20th century, was inspired by the lotus blossom, with 27 marble-clad concrete "petals" clustered in groups of three. It is open to people from all religions.

2. INDIA GATE

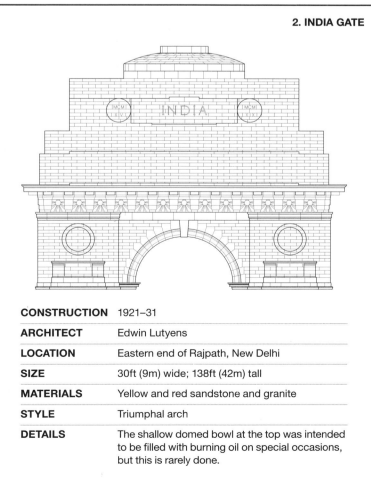

CONSTRUCTION	1921–31
ARCHITECT	Edwin Lutyens
LOCATION	Eastern end of Rajpath, New Delhi
SIZE	30ft (9m) wide; 138ft (42m) tall
MATERIALS	Yellow and red sandstone and granite
STYLE	Triumphal arch
DETAILS	The shallow domed bowl at the top was intended to be filled with burning oil on special occasions, but this is rarely done.

3. HAWA MAHAL

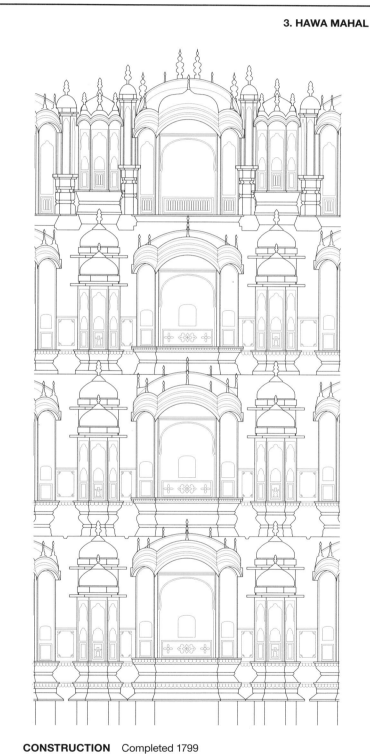

CONSTRUCTION	Completed 1799
ARCHITECT	Lal Chand Ustad
LOCATION	Hawa Mahal Road, Badi Choupad, Jaipur
SIZE	50ft (15m) tall; 5 stories
MATERIALS	Red and pink sandstone
STYLE	Rajput and Mogul
DETAILS	Also known as the Palace of Winds, the Hawa Mahal is part of the women's section of the City Palace complex. The intricate, honeycomb-like facade, shaped to resemble the crown of the Hindu god Krishna, includes 953 small windows where ladies of the royal court could watch the street life below without being seen.

TAJ MAHAL

CONSTRUCTION	1631–54
ARCHITECT	Ustad Ahmad Lahori (aka Isa Khan); Ismail Afandi (aka. Ismail Khan); Isa Muhammad Afandi; etc. (historical records are unclear)
LOCATION	Dharmapuri, Forest Colony, Agra, India
SIZE	180ft (55m) long on each side; dome: 60ft (18m) in diameter; 240ft (73m) tall
MATERIALS	Marble, jasper, jade, and crystal
STYLE	Mogul
DETAILS	Regarded by many to be one of the Seven Wonders of the World, the Taj Mahal was commissioned by the Mogul emperor Shah Jahan as a bejeweled mausoleum for his beloved wife whom he called Mumtaz Mahal (Jewel of the Palace).

Hong Kong

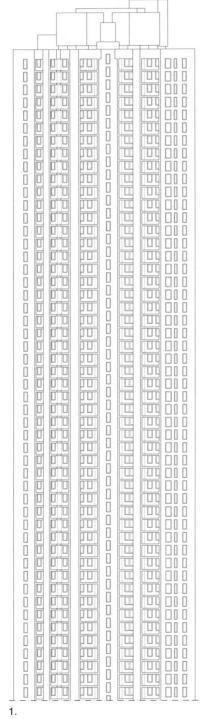

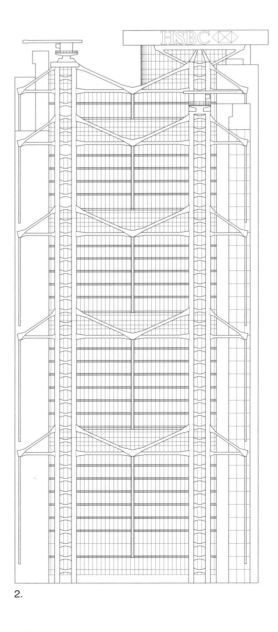

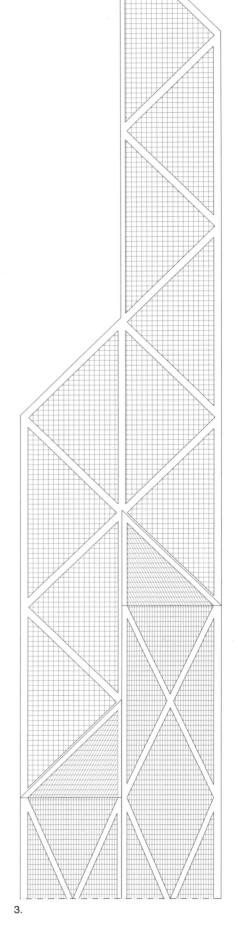

1.

2.

3.

1. HIGH-RISE HOUSING
2. HSBC BUILDING
3. BANK OF CHINA TOWER

Hong Kong developed as a city after the 1842 Opium War between China and Britain. The town had been an important fishing and pearl-trading port in the South China Sea since the 2nd century BCE and became an important trading post for the British who attempted to trade tea for opium in China. Conflict arose when China's emperor banned opium.

After the war and until the early 1900s, Hong Kong developed as a naval base and a trading port for manufactured goods. This development also brought population growth, and Britain leased extra territory, increasing the area of the colony by 90 percent.

The Hong Kong we see today is a result of manufacturing progress and a flight of rich industrialists from Shanghai. The latter created a rapid expansion in industry and banking, but at a cost. Slums had become unsustainable, so in the 1950s Alexander Grantham (Hong Kong's governor) established the "high-rise" plan—the biggest urban housing development in the world. Prefabricated concrete towers rose to heights of 500ft (150m). High-rises not only solved the housing problem but gave international corporations the ability to build tall in a low-tax country, making investment and finance Hong Kong's speciality today.

1. HIGH-RISE HOUSING

CONSTRUCTION	From 1965
ARCHITECT	Various
LOCATION	Metropolitan area
SIZE	Various
MATERIALS	Various
STYLE	Modern
DETAILS	Hong Kong is the sixth-most densely populated city in the world. When the building height restriction was lifted in 1955, high-rise buildings and skyscrapers became the solution.

2. HSBC BUILDING

CONSTRUCTION	1979–86
ARCHITECT	Foster + Partners; Ove Arup & Partners; and Cleveland Bridge UK Ltd. (structural engineers)
LOCATION	1 Queen's Road, Central
SIZE	1,065,627ft^2 (99,000m^2) in area; 587ft (179m) tall; 47 stories
MATERIALS	Glass, steel, and aluminum
STYLE	High-tech/structural Expressionism
DETAILS	The headquarters of the Hong Kong and Shanghai Banking Corporation includes a mirrored "sunscoop" at the top of the 131ft (40m) high atrium that reflects sunlight down through the atrium to the public plaza.

3. BANK OF CHINA TOWER

CONSTRUCTION	1985–90
ARCHITECT	I. M. Pei & Partners, with Sherman Kung & Associates Architects and Thomas Boada S. L.
LOCATION	1 Garden Road, Central
SIZE	1,453,128ft^2 (135,000m^2) in area; 1,205ft (367m) tall; 72 stories
MATERIALS	Steel, glass, granite, concrete, and aluminum
STYLE	High-tech/structural Expressionism
DETAILS	Four triangular towers of varying heights rise from a granite podium that includes water gardens to help mask traffic noise.

Shanghai

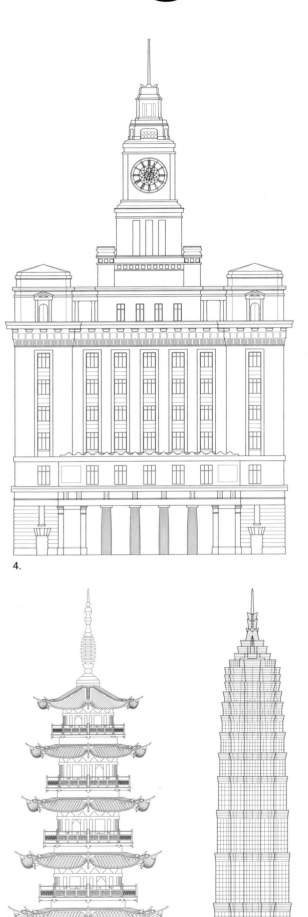

4.

5.

3.

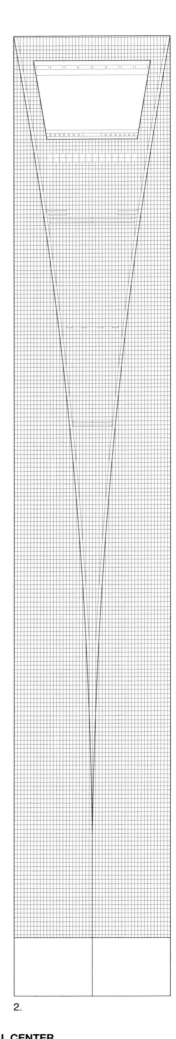

2.

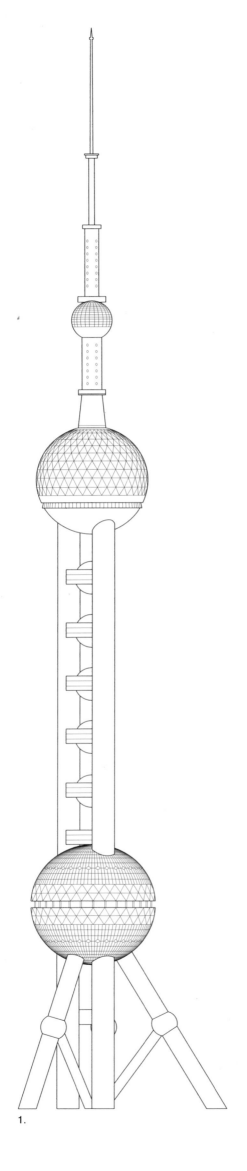

1.

1. ORIENTAL PEARL TOWER 2. SHANGHAI WORLD FINANCIAL CENTER
3. JIN MAO TOWER
4. SHANGHAI CUSTOMS HOUSE
5. LONGHUA PAGODA

Most famous for its recent development in skyscrapers, busy roads full of neon signs, and more than 20 million inhabitants, Shanghai became a walled city in the 16th century to protect its silk and cotton trading port from invasions and immigration. After the first Opium War (1839–42), Shanghai was opened up to British consuls and merchants from France, the US, and Germany, and the city was divided into two segments; one European, the other more traditionally Chinese.

The architecture today is a reflection of this history and blends the two cultures, ranging from the very European Shanghai Customs House to the reconstructed 10th-century Longhua Pagoda.

Today the city is one of the largest in the world, with more skyscrapers than New York. It is the cultural gateway of China, combining the traditions of East and West with a sense of futurism unlike other cities.

1. ORIENTAL PEARL TOWER

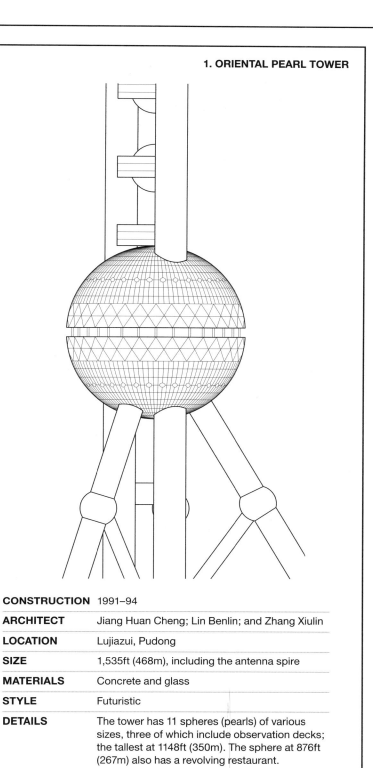

CONSTRUCTION	1991–94
ARCHITECT	Jiang Huan Cheng; Lin Benlin; and Zhang Xiulin
LOCATION	Lujiazui, Pudong
SIZE	1,535ft (468m), including the antenna spire
MATERIALS	Concrete and glass
STYLE	Futuristic
DETAILS	The tower has 11 spheres (pearls) of various sizes, three of which include observation decks; the tallest at 1148ft (350m). The sphere at 876ft (267m) also has a revolving restaurant.

2. SHANGHAI WORLD FINANCIAL CENTER

CONSTRUCTION	1998–2008
ARCHITECT	Kohn Pedersen Fox Associates (KPF); Mori Building Co.; Irie Miyake Architects & Engineers
LOCATION	100 Century Avenue, Pudong New Area
SIZE	1,622ft (494m) tall; 101 stories
MATERIALS	Glass, steel, and stone
STYLE	Contemporary
DETAILS	Described as "a city within the city," the mixed-use tower includes a retail base, 62 floors of offices, and one of the world's highest hotels, occupying floors 79 to 93. The 94th to 100th floors accommodate a visitor center and observation decks.

3. JIN MAO TOWER

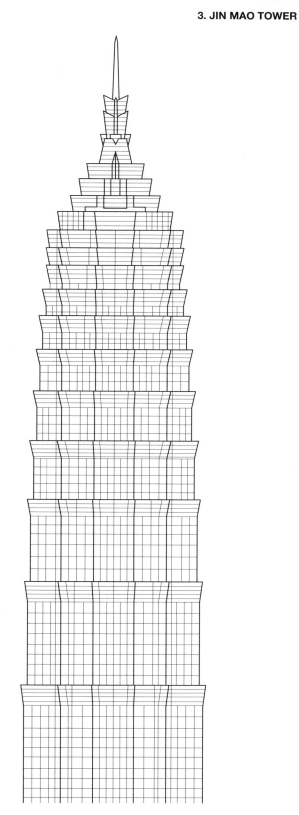

CONSTRUCTION	1994–99
ARCHITECT	Skidmore, Owings & Merrill (SOM), with Shanghai Institute of Architectural Design & Research
LOCATION	88 Century Avenue, Lujiazui
SIZE	1,380ft (421m) tall; 88th (top) floor observatory
MATERIALS	Glass, stainless steel, aluminum, and granite
STYLE	Chinese postmodern
DETAILS	In 2016 a terrifyingly high glass-floored skywalk, only 4ft (1.2m) wide with no guardrail, opened on the 88th floor. It's 1,115ft (340m) high.

4. SHANGHAI CUSTOMS HOUSE

CONSTRUCTION	Completed 1927
ARCHITECT	Palmer & Turner Architects
LOCATION	137 Jiujiang Road, the Bund
SIZE	351,765ft² (32,680m²) in area; 300ft (90m) tall; 11 stories (including clock tower)
MATERIALS	Granite, brick, and marble
STYLE	Neoclassical
DETAILS	The clock and bell mechanisms, based on Big Ben's design specifications, were made in London. The clock faces on the four sides of the tower are each 18ft (5.4m) in diameter.

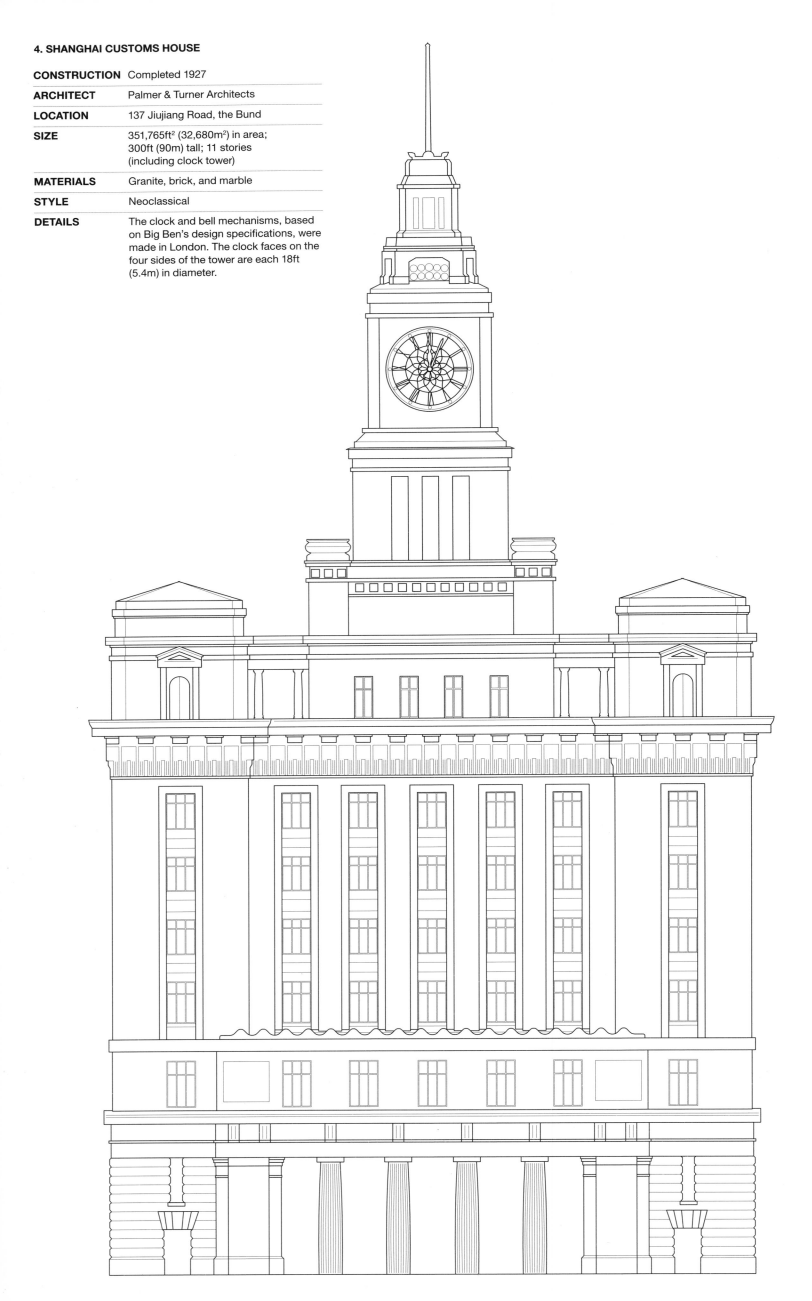

CONSTRUCTION	Completed 242 CE (original); rebuilt 977; restored 1954
ARCHITECT	Various
LOCATION	Longhua Temple, 2853 Longhua Road
SIZE	132ft (40m) tall; 7 stories
MATERIALS	Brick core and wooden exterior
STYLE	Song dynasty pagoda
DETAILS	Part of the Longhua Temple complex, the oldest temple in Shanghai, the only element of the pagoda remaining from the 900s is the brick core. The wooden parts have been rebuilt repeatedly over the centuries.

Tokyo

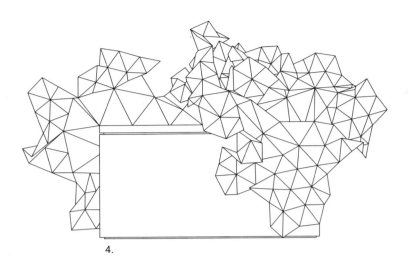

4.

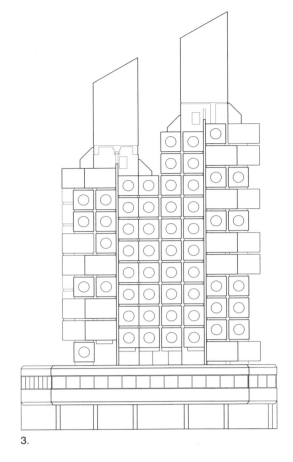

3.

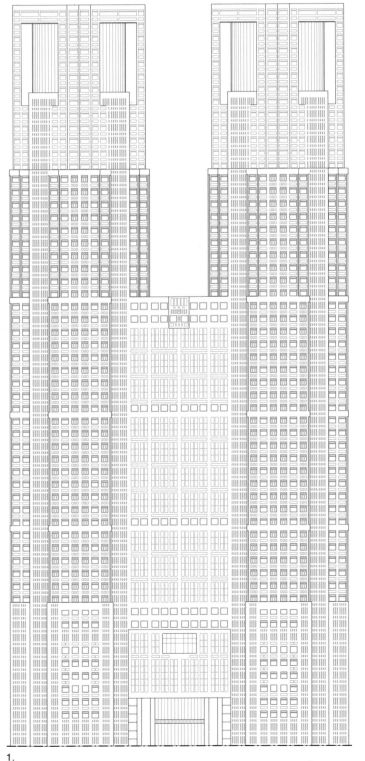

1.

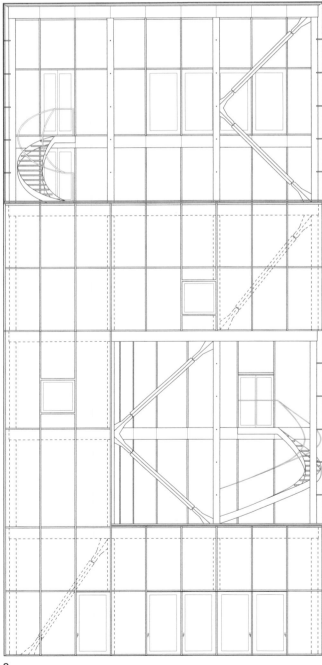

2.

**1. TOKYO METROPOLITAN GOVERNMENT BUILDING NO. 1
2. SHIBAURA HOUSE 3. NAKAGIN CAPSULE TOWER
4. BLOOMBERG PAVILION**

The city of Tokyo, formerly Edo, was founded as a fortified castle in the early 1600s. This site later became the palace of the emperor in the center of Tokyo. From its origins as a military post it evolved though craftsmanship into Japan's most important city for culture and politics, but it did not become the emperor's seat until the Meiji restoration in 1868, when the emperor moved to Edo and renamed it Tokyo—Eastern Capital.

Since then, the ruling powers of Tokyo, and Japan, have been keen to embrace the Western world. The city developed and grew considerably, but at great cost. The city has had substantial and tragic losses due to earthquakes—in 1923 the city lost half of its population and several of its buildings; and it was bombed heavily at the end of World War II. Nevertheless, the city has rebuilt and progressed. Commissions for the most significant buildings are usually awarded to Japanese architects, rather than internationally renowned ones. The Tokyo Metropolitan Government Building, an icon of the city, was designed with a combination of hidden references to traditional Japanese houses, Gothic cathedrals (the two towers), and modern digital technology.

1. TOKYO METROPOLITAN GOVERNMENT BUILDING NO. 1

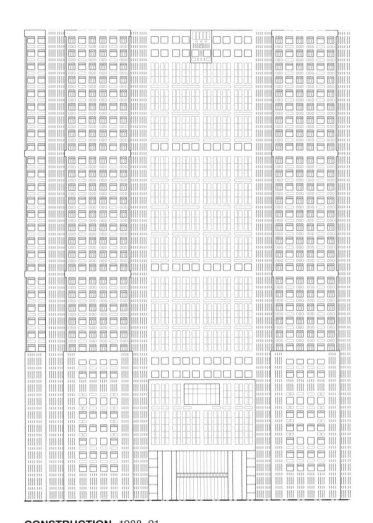

CONSTRUCTION	1988–91
ARCHITECT	Kenzō Tange; Taisei Corporation
LOCATION	2-8-1, Nishi-Shinjuku, Shinjuku-ku
SIZE	2,109,726ft^2 (196,000m^2) in area; 797ft (243m) tall; 48 stories
MATERIALS	Granite, glass, and steel
STYLE	Postmodern
DETAILS	Said to have been inspired by both Gothic cathedrals and computer chips. The observation decks at the top of both towers are open to the public, free of charge.

2. SHIBAURA HOUSE

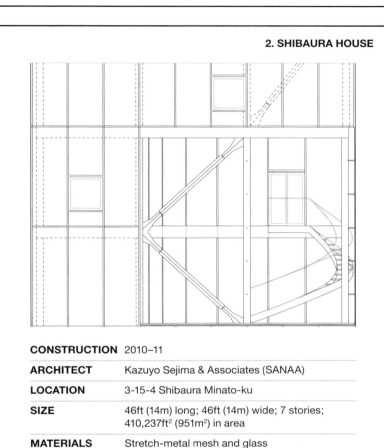

CONSTRUCTION	2010–11
ARCHITECT	Kazuyo Sejima & Associates (SANAA)
LOCATION	3-15-4 Shibaura Minato-ku
SIZE	46ft (14m) long; 46ft (14m) wide; 7 stories; 410,237ft^2 (951m^2) in area
MATERIALS	Stretch-metal mesh and glass
STYLE	Contemporary
DETAILS	The totally transparent building serves as a center for local and international cultural programs and events.

3. NAKAGIN CAPSULE TOWER

CONSTRUCTION	1970–72
ARCHITECT	Kisho Kurokawa Architects & Associates
LOCATION	16-10, Ginza 8, Shimbashi
SIZE	33,271ft^2 (3,091m^2) in area; 177ft (54m) tall; 13 stories; 140 units, each measuring 108ft^2 (10m^2)
MATERIALS	Coated steel, concrete, and CorTen® steel
STYLE	Japanese Metabolism
DETAILS	One of Tokyo's most famous buildings, it is the world's first example of capsule architecture. Its current dilapidated state has it under constant threat of demolition, with preservationists calling for its restoration.

4. BLOOMBERG PAVILION

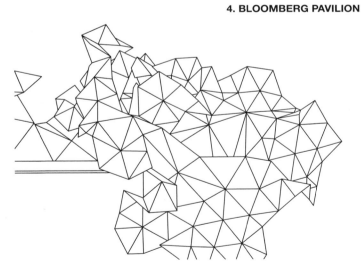

CONSTRUCTION	2011 (it has now been deconstructed)
ARCHITECT	Akihisa Hirata Architecture Office
LOCATION	Museum of Contemporary Art Tokyo, 4-1-1 Miyoshi, Koto-ku
SIZE	248ft^2 (23m^2)
MATERIALS	Coated steel and glass
STYLE	Contemporary and minimalist
DETAILS	This temporary pavilion installed outside the entrance to the museum from late 2011 to October 2012 hosted exhibitions by young artists.

Sydney

1.

2.

3.

1. SYDNEY TOWER
2. QUEEN VICTORIA BUILDING
3. SYDNEY HARBOUR BRIDGE

Famous for its harbor opera house, Sydney developed as a city with the arrival of British convicts and settlers in the late 1700s. The indigenous inhabitants resisted the colonizers but were unable to prevent them from settling in modern day Sydney. The aboriginal people consisted of 29 clans, called the Eora Nation.

The main developments came into place after Governor Macquarie took control in 1809. Since the land was not suitable for cultivation and supplies were scarce, Macquarie engaged in more than 250 urban projects—including roads, bridges, and sanitation—and offered freedom to prisoners who did exemplary work. The first lighthouse was built in the classic style by convict Francis Greenway, who went on to design several other buildings. Many can be seen in the center of the city, along with the Queen Victoria building that was built in Romanesque Revival style.

1. SYDNEY TOWER

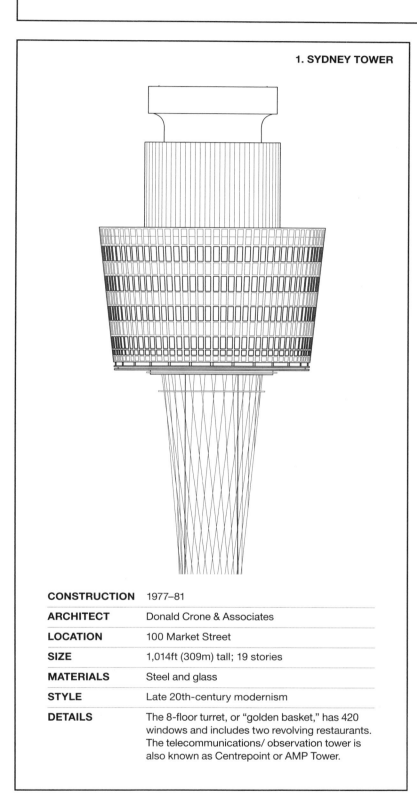

CONSTRUCTION	1977–81
ARCHITECT	Donald Crone & Associates
LOCATION	100 Market Street
SIZE	1,014ft (309m) tall; 19 stories
MATERIALS	Steel and glass
STYLE	Late 20th-century modernism
DETAILS	The 8-floor turret, or "golden basket," has 420 windows and includes two revolving restaurants. The telecommunications/ observation tower is also known as Centrepoint or AMP Tower.

2. QUEEN VICTORIA BUILDING

CONSTRUCTION	1893–98
ARCHITECT	George McRae
LOCATION	429-481 George Street
SIZE	620ft (190m) long; 98ft (30m) wide; 190ft (58m) tall
MATERIALS	Sandstone
STYLE	Romanesque Revival
DETAILS	Also known as QVB, the shopping emporium and concert hall replaced ramshackle market stalls. Remodeled several times and threatened with demolition over the years, it was restored in the mid-1980s and again in 2008. It is now considered a treasured gem of the city, and an upscale shopping adventure.

3. SYDNEY HARBOUR BRIDGE

CONSTRUCTION	1923–32
ENGINEER	John Bradfield (initial design); Ralph Freeman/ Douglas Fox and Partners (final design)
LOCATION	Sydney Harbour
SIZE	3,769ft (1,149m) long; 160ft (48.8m) wide; 440ft (134m) tall
MATERIALS	Steel and pylons made of concrete covered with gray granite
STYLE	Through-arch bridge
DETAILS	Nicknamed "the Coathanger" because of its shape, the bridge carries road, rail, and pedestrian traffic and is particularly known for its spectacular New Year's fireworks display.

SYDNEY OPERA HOUSE

CONSTRUCTION	1959–73
ARCHITECT	Jørn Utzon; completed by Hall, Todd & Littlemore when Utzon resigned in 1966
LOCATION	Bennelong Point, Sydney Harbour
SIZE	607ft (185m) long; 394ft (120m) wide; 220ft (67m) tall (equivalent to 22 stories); covers 4.4ac (1.8ha) of land
MATERIALS	Concrete, granite, glass, and ceramics
STYLE	Expressionist modernism
DETAILS	One of the most recognized structures in the world, the opera house is one of a handful World Heritage buildings to achieve green certification for its eco-friendly operations.

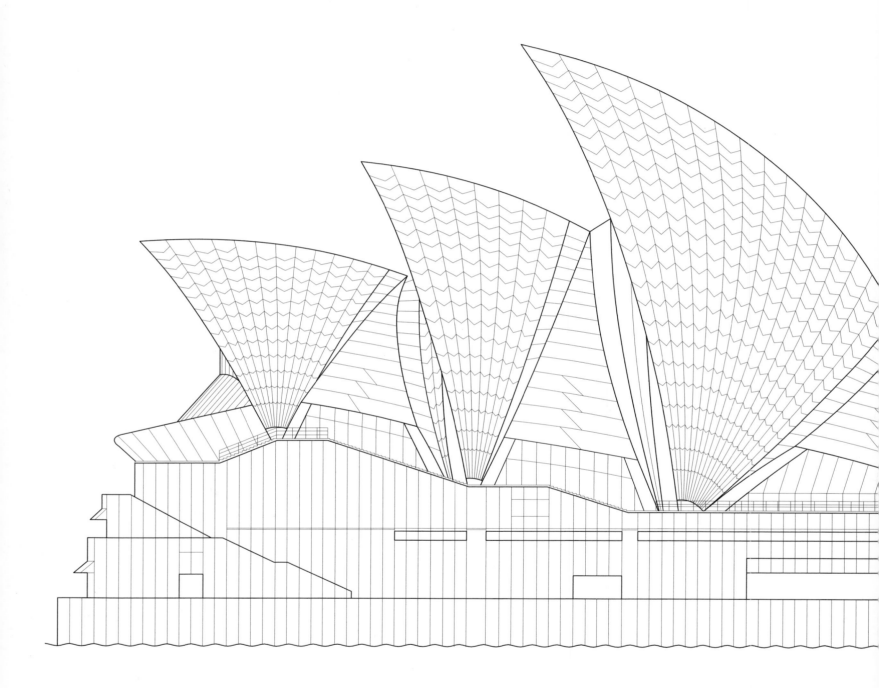

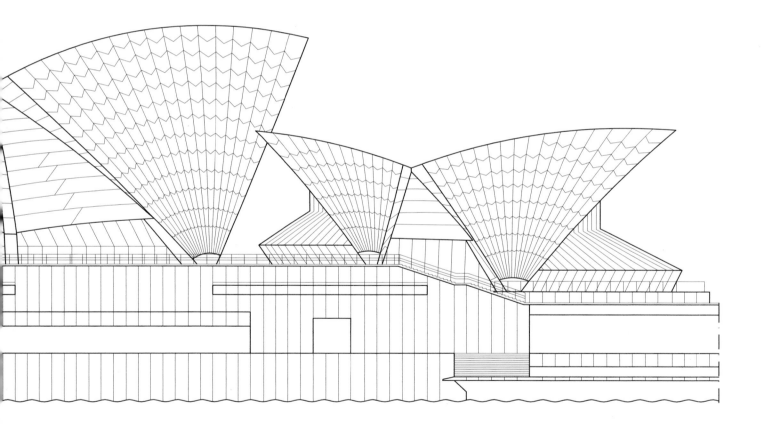

Index

Acknowledgments

We'd like to thank the whole RotoVision team and in particular Abbie Sharman, Alison Morris, Agata Rybicka, Isheeta Mustafi, and Mark Searle for their contributions to this project. Many thanks to Valeria Carnevale and Kristen Richards, Hon. AIA, Hon. ASLA for their contributions as well.

studio esinam

The publishers would like to thank the following contributors for their help researching, compiling, and writing the text:

Kristen Richards, Hon. AIA, Hon. ASLA
Kristen is the Founder and Editor-in-Chief of ArchNewsNow.com, launched in 2002. She served as the editor of *Oculus* magazine, the quarterly journal of the American Institute of Architects New York Chapter from 2003–2016. Previously, she spent two years as editor of DesignArchitecture.com, following a 10-year tenure at *Interiors* magazine as news editor and feature writer.

Valeria Carnevale
Valeria is a senior lecturer in Architecture at University of Derby. She specializes in Architecture and the Built Environment.